MASTER OF THE PIECES

*Being Restored, Redeemed, and Empowered
by the Love of God*

JOELLE MARYN

*This book is dedicated to my grandparents,
Anne and Thomas Amodeo, who saved
my life through their love of God,
the Rosary, and perseverance in prayer.*

CONTENTS

PART 3: RESTORED

APPENDIX

INTRODUCTION

As a model, actress, and CEO, I looked like I had it all. National model, check. Billboard in Times Square, check. International TV host, check. Dream homes on the beach and in the hill country, fancy car, designer clothes, celebrity friends—check, check, check.

Until one day, I finally realized that everything was truly nothing. And by leaving it all, I gained everything. God resurrected my wildest dreams and dreamed new ones for me that were even bigger and more fulfilling than I ever could have imagined. However, to get to this place, I had to be willing to face my brokenness and surrender to Him every single piece that had led me there.

Beginning with a tragic house fire when I was six years old, my life was marked by severe trials and events that left me feeling broken, smashed, and ashamed. Yet to the world, I appeared victorious, powerful, and glamorous. I was becoming an expert at wearing a mask and portraying the image I thought would make me appear more successful. But, despite how I looked on the outside, underneath my worldliness was a lost girl who felt incredibly alone.

To keep up the façade, I also couldn't let others get too close or else they would see the truth. I spent years secretly feeling hopeless and tried to arrange the shattered pieces of my life into something that would make me feel whole. But it seemed as if I could never be put back together again.

The destruction did not happen overnight. It was only after years of feeling chipped away at by the world, others, and my own shame that I didn't even know who I was anymore. I was too busy trying to be who everyone else wanted me to be. And suffering from some sort of spiritual amnesia, I forgot why I was here and wasn't living freely.

However, in 2012, a miraculous encounter with Christ changed everything. The Lord taught me then—and is still teaching me—that He alone is the Master of my pieces. I am whole in Him and only in Him.

Looking back, nothing but God could fill the void I felt inside. I knew I needed healing but didn't know where to turn. So, finally, after much suffering and a life-altering day at a photo shoot in Hollywood, I reached out to the Lord in prayer. I then experienced a dramatic encounter with Him that opened my eyes in extraordinary ways. This led me to turn my life around and begin the journey to live in my true identity as a beloved daughter of God.

Following this event, I returned to the Catholic Church. Subsequently, after a long period of prayer and intense healing, the Lord called me into full-time ministry. I've been an evangelist for several years now, sharing the message of God's healing love, which has radiated hope and purpose in life to millions around the world. As an actress, TV host, speaker, and writer, I also engage in faith-based and family-friendly projects to help lead others closer to Christ.

Have you ever looked in the mirror and not recognized the person looking back? Are you unsure who you are and why you are here? Have you ever felt "not enough," alone, invisible, forgotten, or unloved? Have you felt unsure of how God could forgive and love you after all the things that you've done? If so, this book is for you.

Jesus is the Master of our pieces, and He alone is our healer. None of us go through life unscathed, and at some point, we all forget who we are—that we are loved and belong to Him. If you have ever struggled with rejection, abandonment, grief, or other hurts in life, this book will help you allow Jesus to restore and redeem you.

God promises us that He will work all things together for our good and empowers us to help others. In this book, I share the things that have helped me, and I have faith in God that they will help you too. Trust that you are reading this for a reason, and God's Divine plan for you is glorious. Healing is a process and takes time, but God is faithful and will fulfill His promises. He has given you gifts, talents, and a unique personality specific to the mission He has for you. He wants you to be happy and fully alive for His glory.

My prayer is that as you read this, God touches and heals your heart. He knows what you are going through right now and wants to help you. He wants you to live freely and to know who you are and whose you are. He's waiting for your "yes." Today is the day to choose to let Him in. Open the doors of your heart so His Love and Truth may reign. May you be restored, redeemed, and empowered by His Love.

HOW TO USE THIS BOOK

This book includes personal stories, prayers, Scripture, and reflection questions that will help you invite God into your woundedness so that the healing process can begin. While so many things may seem impossible to us, all things are possible in Christ.

I pray for your heart to be open to hearing what the Lord is saying to you through each chapter. I share some of the most painful, humbling, and joyful moments of my life in hopes that you can relate to some of them.

We all have a story, and God is the only one who knows it in complete depth. He's the only one who can redeem our past, and He has not come to condemn us but to bring His merciful Love to our hearts. He alone is the Master of the pieces.

To begin:

- Invite the Holy Spirit to guide you
- Go at your own pace
- Reflect
- Pray

The book is divided into two main parts: "Shattered" includes a chapter for each broken piece, and "Restored" includes chapters about how God healed and restored each one. Every chapter concludes with "Picking Up the Pieces," which reflects on the chapter's theme. Please go slowly to meditate on the questions and pay attention to what comes to your mind and heart. Do not be afraid of tears or uncomfortable feelings that arise, as they may be pointing you to the area where the Lord is speaking to you.

You may want to read the book several times to go deeper into healing, and it would also be great in a Bible study setting so you can see that you're not alone. Everyone is struggling with something, and God loves you. Remember, there is no such thing as being too broken.

OPENING PRAYER

Lord Jesus, please fill me with your Holy Spirit and guide my thoughts and heart as I read this book. Bring all of my darkness to the light and heal me in any way that is needed: mind, heart, body, and soul. Please restore, redeem, and empower me to do your will. Let me hear you speaking to me and help me know who I truly am so that I may love and serve you better. Amen.

PART 1

THE TURNING POINT

CHAPTER 1

REPENTANCE AND FAITH

For I know well the plans I have in mind for you—
oracle of the LORD—plans for your welfare and not
for woe, so as to give you a future of hope.
—Jeremiah 29:11

Before I share about the fire that nearly destroyed my life, I want to rewind to eleven years ago and share about the day a new fire began to rage around and within me. This fire was the beginning of change—a much-needed change that started to bring light to help me see my situation more clearly.

In reality, my biggest high was my biggest low. Paradoxically, despite appearances, the more I was "known," I actually felt "unknown," and the more I had, the less I really had. Since the things of the world are not what make us special or define us, they will never satisfy the deepest desires in our hearts.

At this point in my life, I was dealing with a tremendous amount of brokenness and was in great need of healing, but I had no idea how it was possible. While God never left me, I had certainly turned my back on Him as I was seeking healing and love in all the wrong places and faces.

My brokenness was so deep and excruciatingly painful. Though I smiled for the cameras, I felt like a fake—not a true masterpiece. Instead, it seemed my life was in pieces and could never be made whole again. My exterior had become a colorful and detailed portrait of who I thought others wanted me to be.

I also learned that many people don't tend to love you when you are at your lowest, but oh, how many "friends" you have at the top! Sadly, that's what I experienced. Many wanted to be my "friend" but didn't really care to know who I was inside. I was treated as an object, a something rather than a someone.

This is how I was feeling when I went out to Los Angeles for a supposed dream-come-true photoshoot. As a model and the face of a cosmetic company, I may have appeared triumphant, but I was just out there checking another box.

Standing on a rooftop of an exquisite, tall building wearing an expensive designer dress with the Hollywood sign behind me, I seemed like I was on top of the world. The gown was long, black, and strapless with layers of silk, chiffon, and lace. Belted with sparkling crystals and satin ribbon, it reminded me of something a fairy-tale princess would wear.

My skin glistened in the sun, as one of the top artists in Los Angeles touched up my makeup. As I did several poses in front of the camera, each seemed more meaningless than the last. I thought, *What am I selling? Where am I heading?*

As I held a compact for one of the photos, I saw my reflection and barely recognized myself. *Who is this woman looking back at me? What is her purpose in life? Could this really be it? If this is my mountaintop moment, why does it feel so meaningless? Who am I taking with me on this journey to nothingness?*

To make matters worse, I had vertigo and felt so dizzy. And as if the top of the building wasn't high enough, the photographer positioned me on a ledge near the center of the rooftop, which I almost fell off several times. Maybe it wasn't vertigo after all. Perhaps I was just so tired, dizzy, and confused from being caught up in a life without meaning.

While I made it through the shoot, there was a moment on the rooftop when the sun hit me just right and a new warmth began to fill me. It was the beginning of a cry for help in my heart that continued to grow throughout the rest of the day.

Then, later that evening, I was mingling on Rodeo Drive with celebrities. However, instead of feeling successful, I felt lost and empty, as if I didn't even exist or have a reason to. I had checked every box of anything I ever thought I wanted in life but had no idea who I was. It was like I had completely lost my identity, and it was exhausting to maintain the perfect image all the time.

As the night went on, several temptations presented themselves to me, and every direction I turned felt unsafe. After one of my celebrity friends left, I found myself at the hotel bar with a famous, handsome drummer who had just played onstage at the Grammy Awards. He was trying to lure me to go somewhere with him, and his intentions of what that entailed were made clear. I can't believe I even flirted with the idea, but the thoughts ping-ponged in my head as to what I should do. I felt like I was under a spell and have no idea how I escaped the situation.

At that moment, I didn't trust myself or anyone else and wasn't sure what was real anymore. I thought, *Does anyone really love me or even know me? Do I even love and know myself?* I so desperately wanted to be known and longed to be loved, but not for what's on the surface. Rather, I wanted to be loved for who I was inside—the person that even I didn't know anymore.

Eventually, I got back to my hotel room around 2:00 a.m., feeling at an all-time low. I was confused, disoriented, and upset. Bursting into tears, I spent the rest of the night naked on the shower floor. I felt ashamed, alone, and completely annihilated. It seemed like I was in there for hours, crying and opening my heart.

I was genuinely reaching out to God for the first time in many years. My prayers had been so shallow up to that moment. I would pray, "Lord, can I have this? Can I have that? I want this! I want that!" Never a conversation, not a relationship, not asking Him what was best, but rather, "Lord, here's my plan, I know what I want. Please give it to me." I had treated God like a personal assistant as my true gods were makeup and fame—but look where they had gotten me. I had never felt worse about myself and wanted to run and hide. However, there was nowhere to go. Begging God with all of my heart and pleading for help, I finally prayed, "Lord, please help me. I need you."

When I finally got out of the shower, I noticed the drain was imprinted on my knees. Then, I caught a glimpse of myself in the mirror. If anyone could see a side-by-side picture of me from earlier that day in my fancy dress with my flawless makeup on and compare it to my tear-stained eyes later that night, I would be unrecognizable.

With black mascara streaming down my face, fake eyelashes half on and half off, I looked far from any picture of beauty. My eyes were all red from crying. My hair was dripping wet and stringy from the heat products that had been used on it that day. However, something new had begun pulsing in my heart. My outside and my inside were being purified, and my cry for help had opened the door to grace.

My grandparents and family had been praying for years that I would come back to the Lord and the Catholic Church. They persevered in faith and never gave up on me. I know it was from their intercessions that this saving grace had begun. Just the fact that I admitted my brokenness and had finally asked for help was an enormous blessing.

I also began to sense that God had a purpose for my life and that I was created for something much deeper. I had always felt that He wanted to use me but never asked Him how or made myself available.

Although not all my desires were "bad," they were certainly misdirected. I was too busy trying to attain what I thought was true, good, and beautiful. But it all turned out to be a web of lies—nothing but false, distorted beauty that led to shame. There's only one truth, and that truth sets us free. That night was the beginning of my freedom and a new life in Christ.

 PICKING UP THE PIECES

Have you ever thought you had it all together and tried to tell God the way you think things should go? Have you ever looked in the mirror and felt like what you see doesn't match how you feel on the inside? Are you ready to cry out and open your heart to hear the plans that God has for you?

PRAYER

Lord Jesus, please help me to know who I am in you, why I am here, and what your plan is for my life. I come to you with an open heart and a desire to hear your voice. Please guide me, strengthen me, and console me. Help me to know, love, and serve you better. Please, Lord, help pick up the pieces. Please restore, redeem, and empower me. Amen.

CHAPTER 2

TRUTH AND LOVE

Above all, let your love for one another be intense,
because love covers a multitude of sins.
—1 Peter 4:8

With an open heart for God's will, I returned home to Texas from Los Angeles. Then, about a week later, I was walking through my large, Tuscan-styled bathroom toward my closet. Something stopped me dead in my tracks, and it's hard to explain the depths of what happened. Actually, I believe it's impossible to ever describe its full depth. However, I will share what I can.

It was a mystical experience, some sort of an illumination of the state of my soul, and I was alarmed at what I saw. I have heard of something similar happening to people who almost died on an operating table, but here I was—wide awake.

As truth penetrated my soul, it left me in a spiritual pain much greater than any physical pain I've ever known. Shocked and horrified, I dropped to the floor with my mouth wide open as my entire life flashed before my eyes, in what appeared to be columns. In the first column to the left, I saw every sin I had ever committed and its effects on others. Things that I had not even understood in my blindness were wrong, I could now see in full light. I thought, *How can this be? How could I have been so lost? How could I have misled so many people toward the lure of worldly things?*

I saw how others followed me and how others followed them. It went on and on. My actions created a ripple effect that went many layers deep. I had no idea of my influence, yet I realized I was leading people in the wrong direction. And the pain I felt in seeing my selfishness and its effects on others was terrifying.

I had spent so much time captivated by vanity and idolizing beauty rather than giving thanks to God for it. Caught up in the false things of the world, I was misusing my beauty and teaching others to misuse theirs, especially through the sin of immodesty.

The worst part of what I was shown was my "good" column, which was to the right. It was nearly empty—I was crushed. This column was for loving others and using the gifts I had been given to help build the kingdom of God.

In this moment, my eyes were opened, and I saw I wasn't being who God created me to be. Sins of omission are real, and I had wasted so many gifts and graces that were supposed to be used to help others. And while my story is one of mercy, during this experience I felt that I deserved hell.

Although, interestingly enough, the day prior, I thought I had a free ticket to heaven, and anyone who knew me didn't think I was a "bad person" either. I was even singing in a non-denominational Christian band at the time, but the problem was that I was the idol of worship. My gifts and desires were glorifying me, not God.

Last, the Holy Spirit showed me that the good column weighed more than my worst sin. There are no words that can describe my pain in seeing that I hadn't loved God, others, or myself how I should have. Right then, I understood that the most significant weight of our judgment is on love.

Saint John of the Cross said, "In the evening of life, we will be judged on love alone." If we love God, others, and ourselves, how can we sin? If we are being who God created us to be and using the gifts He gave us for His glory, then we are living in His light and are filled with joy. Without knowing the Scriptures at the time, I saw in full truth that love indeed "covers a multitude of sins" (1 Peter 4:8).

God is love and deserves our whole heart, not just a piece of us when we feel like it's convenient to talk to Him. I was unhappy and knew something was wrong. However, I couldn't see it clearly for what it was before this experience because I had been so blind. But now, my eyes were restored, and my life was changed forever.

It took me nearly two years to figure out what it even meant. Eventually, I learned of some saints who had described a similar experience and called it an "illumination of conscience." It was like a preview of the judgment we will all receive after death and what will be revealed at Jesus's second coming.

"When He comes at the end of time to judge the living and the dead, the glorious Christ will reveal the secret disposition of hearts and will render to each man according to his works, and according to his acceptance or refusal of grace."
—*Catechism of the Catholic Church, The Profession of Faith*[1]

Saint Maria Faustina details her encounter with God in her *Diary: Divine Mercy in My Soul.*[2] "Suddenly, I saw the complete condition of my soul as God sees it. I could clearly see all that is displeasing to God. I did not know that even the smallest transgressions will have to be accounted for. What a moment! Who can describe it? To stand before the Thrice-Holy-God!"

I certainly was far from being a saint and sometimes wonder why I received this grace before death. It definitely wasn't earned but seemed to me that I had hit a spiritual rock bottom with nowhere to go but up. It was also clear to me that the Lord was calling me to lead people to Him and not away from Him. He gave me this message to give to others, and I share this encounter of mercy, because now is the time to live and the time to love. There is no other time but now, and I would never wish the pain I experienced on anyone.

I'm very grateful to have received a second chance, as we all do every day. And the beauty of this message and what I have experienced is that God doesn't leave us in our sin. He doesn't give us light to condemn us. He is merciful and gives us grace along with the light. He gives us gifts to help others so that we can be who He created us to be. He makes it so that a fire can't destroy our lives, but a fire can save it. That day He put a new fire in me. It's a fire that cannot be put out, a fire that no one can take from me, a fire that burns but doesn't consume, a fire that heals, and a fire that purifies. It's not the fire of death but the fire of life.

We all have a purpose, and God has a plan for each one of us. No matter how far astray we've gone, and no matter how lost we've become, all can be redeemed. Everything can be turned around and used for the greater good.

May God open our eyes to see our soul how He sees it, and may we spend our time on earth doing His will. Let us live each day like it's our last, so that when we face Him at our death, we have no regrets in this life and have fulfilled our purpose and mission to love.

♡ PICKING UP THE PIECES

How may you be blinded by sin? Are you aware that God has given you gifts and that you are called to use them to help others? How are you filling your good column?

PRAYER

Dear Jesus, please give us light to see our sins so that we may truly repent and turn away from all things that offend you. Please help us to know the gifts you've given us and guide us on how to use them to bring you glory. Thank you for your eternal love and mercy. Amen.

PART 2

SHATTERED

CHAPTER 3

GRIEF

When you pass through waters, I will be with you; through rivers,
you shall not be swept away. When you walk through fire, you shall
not be burned, nor will flames consume you.
—Isaiah 43:2

When I look back, I can look forward because I put my hope in the Master of the pieces of my life. But let me return to the beginning, to the first fire that started it all.

When I was six years old, living in New York, I had a terrible dream that my house was on fire and my mother was going to die. While dreaming, I prayed, "No, Lord, please don't let my mommy die," and she was saved. I woke up so relieved that it was just a dream. The next night, though, I had another dream about a house fire, and this time, my father was going to die.

Again, I prayed, "No, Lord, please don't let my daddy die," and he was saved. Waking up, I felt incredibly relieved that it was just a repeated dream. But during the day, the image of fire continued to flash in my mind, and being a little girl, I was terrified. I didn't know when and if a fire was actually going to happen. I remember being in the bathtub during the day, thinking, *If it happens right now, I would be embarrassed to have to run outside in a towel.* So, I finished my bath as fast as I could.

On the third night, December 18, just before I went to bed, I thought, *What if it happens tonight? It's so cold outside. What if there really is a fire?* So that night I put on a long wool nightgown embroidered with roses. It was kind of itchy, and the little bow on the front of it bothered me, but it was much warmer than my father's white T-shirt that I normally wore to bed. I went to sleep, and again dreamed of fire. This time my sister was going to die, so I started to pray, "No, Lord, please don't let Maria . . ." And before I could say the word "die," I awoke to the sound of roaring flames and my father screaming at the top of his lungs, "Joelle, Joelle, get out! Joelle, there's a fire! Come here!"

I could barely hear what he was saying and couldn't see him at all as the house was filled with clouds of dark smoke. However, I did my best to follow his voice and finally found my way to him. As I jumped into his arms, he carried me through the flames, and I was not burned.

Then he fiercely ran through the hallway toward my sister's room and put me down. I watched as he wildly tried to reach her, but flames surrounded Maria's door and began to scorch his arms. He wasn't making any progress, and we were struggling to breathe.

Since my mother was at a play rehearsal, my father needed my help and shouted for me to run to the neighbor's house. We had a walk-out basement and it was the only way left to get out. In his angst, my father literally threw me down the basement stairs. I fell quickly and with so much force that I thought I would break my neck or die right then and there. But halfway down, something caught me—to this day, I believe it was my guardian angel. And as I was carried down the rest of the stairs very slowly, I felt like I was in a cloud of peace. My feet never even touched the steps. Amid this chaos and the flames, I was somehow brought to safety.

However, when I got to the bottom of the stairs and looked around the pitch-black basement, I was afraid to go to the neighbor's house by myself. I screamed for my father, and he came down and ran out of the house with me. He told me to go next door and get help, and then I watched him run back in. As I stood on the street corner between my house and the neighbor's, I was still horrified at what was happening, and a deep fear crept over me. As I watched my home become engulfed in flames, I thought, *Do I go get help, or do I go back in and try to save my daddy?* I had seen that he wasn't able to get into Maria's room and feared he would die trying.

I decided to run back into the burning house, and when I found my father again, he was very angry with me. But I got him out and convinced him to come with me to get help from the neighbors. When we got there, the emergency call would not go through, and we tried over and over again. Then, just as all seemed hopeless, we finally got connected, and the fire truck arrived in a matter of minutes—time was of the essence.

When the firemen arrived, my father was frantically screaming, "My baby is in there, my baby is in there!" Maria was eleven years old at the time, but in this moment of despair, he referred to her as his "baby." She was his little girl, and his heart ached to go in with the firefighters to get her. However, it was too hot and dangerous, and he didn't have on the proper gear.

Desperate for a solution, he drenched himself in ice-cold water from an outside hose to try not to catch on fire and bear the heat. Then he began running toward the house, but several men held him back and wouldn't let him go in. He was screaming and wanted to help save her, but there was no way he could have survived the conditions. There were now more flames than structure left to the home.

The firefighters rushed in with no time to spare and speedily searched for a baby or child. Then they finally found her: a beautiful, angelic-looking girl, tall with blonde hair, blue eyes, and snow-white skin. She was unconscious, lying on the floor by her bedroom door; she wasn't burned, but was only faintly breathing. They immediately took her to the hospital via ambulance.

My father and I also went for treatment due to smoke inhalation, because we couldn't stop coughing. They gave us oxygen masks and bandaged up my father's arms, which had burns all over them from trying to get to Maria.

I will never forget being in the hospital room with him as we waited to hear about my sister's condition. I was praying in my heart and begging with my entire being, "Lord, please, please don't let Maria die. Please, Lord, please don't let us lose her. Please save her."

But then, the most terrible thing that ever could have happened did. The doctor came in and told us that Maria didn't make it. The damage in her lungs was too extensive, and her heart gave out. They had tried to revive her and got her heart beating for a moment, but then it stopped again.

My father wailed and screamed as he ran over to me and clutched on for dear life. Coupled with losing my sister, seeing my father in so much pain and heartbreak shattered my young spirit. In that grief-stricken moment, I knew our lives were changed forever. I didn't understand precisely how, but I knew things would never be the same.

Before the fire, I had told my mom about the dreams, but we didn't know what they meant until it was too late. And I shared the miraculous experience that happened on the stairs with my family and the news reporter later that week. But being so young and completely devastated, I couldn't comprehend any of it and bitterly questioned God, "Why did this happen? Why was I saved, and why was she not?"

When I asked a nun this question, she said, "Maria is in a better place in heaven. It's so amazing there, and you'll be reunited with her one day." Then I was angry. I thought, *If heaven is so amazing and so great, then why didn't God take me too? Was I not good enough for heaven?* No matter how I looked at it, there was pain. I was either stuck here without her or missing out on the awesomeness of heaven. I wondered, *Does God love me? Why didn't He answer my prayer? Why would such a good God take away my only sister and leave my family in such heartache?*

Have you ever been in shock or disbelief where you raised your eyes to heaven and said, "Seriously, why did you allow this to happen, God? Why now? Why me? Why this?" Are you struggling with a past hurt right now that you know it's time to let go of and give to the Lord? Is it too painful to hold onto anymore?

We have all encountered grief in some way at some time, whether it be the loss of a person, relationship, job, or dream. But God is our healer and can redeem the most terrible and tragic things that have ever happened to us.

It took me many years to begin to surrender my grief to God and to hear His response. I wish I knew then how to let it go and how to let His truth sink in. I wish I had a deeper understanding of His love for us.

I think of Mary Magdalene, being lost in loss at the tomb of our Lord. She was grieving, and understandably so. We experience grief because of the deep love that is rooted in our hearts. Life is precious, and we are created for relationship and communion with one another. When death enters our lives in various ways, we feel the pain so profoundly. It's a process to give our suffering to Jesus and unite it with His cross.

Often, we feel alone and forget that He is with us. It reminds me how Mary Magdalene didn't realize Jesus was speaking to her at the tomb. She thought He was someone else, and only when He called her by name did she recognize Him (John 20:16). This intimacy immediately restored her and gave her hope for the future. He let her know that He cared for her, and He called her to leave the tomb to share the good news. He asked her to let go so that He could ascend.

While we aren't promised a life here without suffering, we are promised that God is with us and will empower us to get through.

We can rise from the ashes with Christ because He knows our name and purpose in life. He has plans for us.

When we are too focused on grief, we can't see or hear Him. Our prayers can seem unheard or unanswered, and the pain can overtake us. We may feel left behind or forgotten.

The enemy loves to take advantage of these moments of human weakness and we often get entangled in the lies of hopelessness, despair, depression, and purposelessness. We can begin to blame ourselves for the loss or live in fear of losing more.

We may even develop a distorted image of God as if He's mean and wants to take everything and everyone away from us. In these moments, it can become difficult to trust that He has a plan and that there is more to life.

At the time, I had no idea that although a fire nearly took my life and stole so much from me, one day, another fire would save it—the fire of the Holy Spirit. But it took many years of searching, doubting, and failing until I finally realized that God can turn even our worst situations for good. He loves us much more than we can ever understand.

 PICKING UP THE PIECES

What trials or tragedies have happened in your life that made you question God's love for you? Have you ever prayed, "God, where were you? Do you love me? Why did you let this happen?" How can you release that pain to the Lord? Can you give it to Him and hear Him say, "I am with you, and I never left you. I cried with you, and I didn't desire these terrible things to happen to you. But I will bring good from it and beauty from the ashes. I will help you turn your pain into your passion. I will help you help others, and no matter what the fire is in your life that nearly took it, I will give you a new fire—the fire of love, the fire of truth, the fire of light, the fire of goodness, and the fire of redemption."

PRAYER

Dear Lord, I'm so sorry for the times I've blamed you for all the bad things that have happened to me. Although you don't need forgiveness, I forgive you for allowing me to be in these terrible situations and release the pain I've been carrying to you. I want to be made new in you. I open my heart to receive your love, truth, and the fire of your Holy Spirit. Jesus, I surrender myself to you. Jesus, I trust in you. Amen.

CHAPTER 4

LOSS

Jesus told her, "I am the resurrection and the life; whoever
believes in me, even if he dies, will live."
—John 11:25

My seventh birthday was three months after the fire. So much grief, confusion, and despair raged in our family. My mother struggled with chronic depression, and although she is a very good person, she was not able to be there for much of my childhood. She lived in deep regret, blaming herself for not having been home the night of the fire.

My father, who recently passed away, had also blamed himself for not being able to save my sister. Misery, along with self-hatred, devoured him. I always felt like he may have secretly blamed me as well for saving him. Although I know that deep down he loved me, I think he wished he had died that night with Maria.

After this tragedy, he spent so many hours at work that I barely saw him. When he was home, he drank a lot of gin and tonic to try to numb the pain. For the rest of his life, he suffered greatly. He was a tortured soul and couldn't fall asleep unless the TV was blaring because he was afraid to be alone with his thoughts. Even in his last years, my mother would often hear him crying loudly at night, "It wasn't my fault, it wasn't my fault."

The fire completely turned our lives upside down, and the sadness and darkness in our family penetrated the deepest recesses of my heart. It was like the heavy clouds of smoke continued to hover over our home. What we couldn't see with our eyes anymore, our spirits could feel.

I suffered a new profound loneliness that seemed to surround and entomb me. I realized that I could no longer talk to Maria and ask her even ordinary things like to go for a bike ride or play a game. I had taken so many things for granted and didn't realize how every moment had been so precious. Even the small, simple things we do in life become such cherished memories.

After her death, my parents and I were not truly living anymore. We were just going through the motions. I had lost everything in the fire—my clothes, toys, house, and sister. Emotionally, it seemed like I had lost my entire family too.

Because of this, three months later on my seventh birthday, I felt compelled to try to do something. I had an amazing idea—or so I thought. We had been staying at my grandmother's house while building a new home, and I was upstairs in the guest room with my new prized possessions—dolls that people had donated to try to make me feel better. But my favorite doll of all was one of my sister's that had been saved from the fire. Although it was covered with black marks and had a terrible musty smell, I treasured it because it was hers. Since I had nothing else to offer God but these dolls, I decided to lay them out on my bed. Then, I made them into the shape and size of Maria.

Without realizing it at the time, it was as if I was making an altar of sacrifice and saying, "Lord, I will give you all that I have if you will give me my sister back." I believed in God's love with such a childlike faith and knew He could raise the dead. So, I reasoned, if He truly loved me, if He truly, truly loved me, then He could understand my pain and the hurt inside and bring Maria back.

As I stood over the dolls, I began praying with all of my heart. I waited, but nothing happened, and the dolls just remained there. I still had hope, so I prayed for a second time, just in case God didn't hear me the first time. Staring intensely at the dolls, I expected the prayer to work, but again, nothing happened. Then I prayed for a third time, beginning to doubt a little bit, but still hoping. However, nothing happened—at least from what I could see.

And in that moment, I felt for the first time that God didn't love me. I knew that He had the power to raise the dead, and I believed that if He loved me, He would have done it. So, without realizing it, I unplugged my phone line to Him, which was prayer. I still prayed, but not like before—not with that childlike hope and faith that could move mountains.

I didn't believe in miracles anymore but still went to church and said some shallow prayers at night. My prayers were motivated by fear. I would beg, "Lord, please protect me and my family . . .

please protect us," because truthfully, I felt so unprotected. It didn't feel safe to live in a world where everything and everyone could be taken away from me at any moment.

Has your life ever been burned down to the ground? Have you been in a position where you feel like, in a way, you've lost everything? Have you struggled to understand why things didn't work out differently? Why the miracle didn't happen the way you wanted it to? Have you ever disconnected your phone line to God and stopped praying?

When something terrible happens to us, we have two choices we can make. One is to draw closer to God and pray despite how we feel. The other choice is to pull away from Him, which lets doubt and fear enter in. The problem with the second option is that we never get out of the tomb. Jesus is calling us and calling our name, but we can't hear Him in these times. And we won't be able to know our mission in life until we can hear His voice again to direct us. Enclosed in the tomb, we can't see the light.

When things don't happen according to how we envisioned them, we can begin to think that God doesn't love us. However, He promises to work all things for good. He finds a way to draw benefit and love out of all our life experiences.

If we look closely and go back to these times of trial, we will begin to see how we were never alone. Many times, God feels far away, but we need to realize in these moments, He is closer than we could ever imagine. We can choose to make a simple act of faith and say to the Lord: "I do believe, help my unbelief!" (Mark 9:24).

Prayer is what reconnects us to the heart of God, and although we may not see those we've lost, they are still with us—praying for us, crying with us, smiling with us, and encouraging us.

Let us keep our eyes fixed on heaven, on the hope of heaven, and the communion of saints. And whenever we feel lost, let us remember that it's never too late to be found. We can choose to hold onto the pain and become stuck, bitter, angry, and resentful. Or we can acknowledge the suffering and begin to give it to God. We can choose to invite Him into our wounds.

I thank God for my sister, Maria, who I believe is in heaven praying for all of us right now and interceding for God's love to heal us.

"Therefore, since we are surrounded by so great a cloud of witnesses, let us rid ourselves of every burden and sin that clings to us and persevere in running the race that lies before us while keeping our eyes fixed on Jesus, the leader, and perfecter of faith."
—Hebrews 12:1–2

♡ PICKING UP THE PIECES

Have you ever lost someone and been stuck in the "whys"? Why, Lord? Why now? Why this way? Picture Jesus with you in that moment, crying with you and holding you in His arms. Hear Him say, "I am with you, and I will make all things new. I love you and will never leave you."

PRAYER

Lord Jesus, you say we just need faith the size of a mustard seed to move a mountain. Please increase our faith and help us to keep our eyes fixed on you. Please comfort us in our afflictions and heal our memories so that no matter what has happened in the past, we can see that you are always with us and never leave us. Thank you for bringing beauty from the ashes. Amen.

CHAPTER 5

REJECTION AND ABANDONMENT

He will wipe every tear from their eyes, and there shall
be no more death or mourning, wailing or pain,
[for] the old order has passed away.
—Revelation 21:4

We rebuilt a home on the same land, but I dreaded the chaos and misery within. My parents often fought ferociously, and I would be forced to be in the middle of them thousands of times trying to break up their arguments. I took on the role of a parent, wanting to get them to stop and be nice to each other.

Usually, I would stick up for one of them, depending on who started the fight and what it was about. On the days when I took my father's side, my mom would get angry with me and say, "You're no good, just like your father."

I must have heard these words hundreds of times over the years. And each time, they pierced my heart as I began to live in the identity that I was no good, and that my father was no good. Unknowingly, I projected this image onto our Heavenly Father as well, and lost sight of His goodness.

By the grace of God, some healing has taken place in my relationship with my parents. Those who know my mother adore her as she's vibrant and outgoing. She is generous and loves to help people when she is well. But sometimes, when we are in grief and pain, we can say and do things that are out of character. Woundedness can blind us. Also, I want to note that my mother is aware of the things I'm sharing in this book and has given her consent in hopes that this writing helps others.

My dad was always a very quiet man with a fragile heart, although what he displayed on the outside seemed cold and harsh. He wasn't shown much love growing up and didn't know how to be affectionate. He didn't speak words that lifted people up and had so much anger inside that he was like a ticking time bomb, which often made it difficult for others to be around him. He was still searching for truth and meaning in life. Above all, his search was for Love, as it is for all of us. My dad was also aware that I would be sharing the truth and reality of my childhood in this book.

One of the saddest things I recently experienced as my father lay on his deathbed was the realization that he hadn't truly lived. I forgave him and asked his forgiveness for anything I ever did to hurt him as well. Filled with a special grace from God, I was able to see him in a new light. I realized this man was a child of God and the Lord had a plan for his life that went unfulfilled. Self-hatred, resentment, fear, and lies dominated his mind and stole his life. However, God's mercy is without bounds, and my father received the last rites. A priest prayed for and anointed him, and I trust in God's love for him.

I share all these things in compassion, as I can't imagine what my parents suffered in the loss of their daughter. I only know my own suffering, which took me years to overcome. That said, I'm not one to sugarcoat things, and I don't want to justify the situation. Fierce anger dominated my childhood home, and I lived in a verbally and emotionally abusive environment. At times, objects and chairs would be thrown, and I certainly never felt safe. I had to fend for myself and would turn into a monster of rage when I witnessed my parents' fights or when hurtful words were said to me. It was unbearable and I felt as if I was being torn into pieces.

Whenever possible, I escaped down the street to the refuge of my grandparents' house. I was blessed to come from a big, loving Italian family on my mother's side, and I had a special relationship with my grandparents, aunts, uncles, and cousins, all of whom I love very much.

Luckily, Grandma and Poppy lived just four doors away. They were devout Catholics and walking into their home felt like receiving a big hug from God. You could feel His love so profoundly there. Pictures of Jesus and Our Lady were all over the walls, along with scores of family photos that had captured good memories. I longed to live with my grandparents as my own home felt like a prison. And although I never told them that, I didn't need to, because everyone in the family could see my parents' unhappiness.

Also, because of the depression and darkness in my home from the loss of my sister, I forgot that I was God's beloved daughter who was made for a purpose. Life became meaningless, and I searched desperately for ways to hide or escape from it.

Sadly, my mother blamed herself for being at the theater the night of the fire. She thought my sister died due to her commitment there. Because of this, she figured she needed to dedicate her life to it. Of course, this was not true as Maria's death was not her fault. However, in her mind, somehow it made sense, and she decided to open a theater company. On the days when she wasn't depressed and in bed, she threw herself into the theater to escape her pain. I quickly followed suit and struggled to earn her love, as the only attention I received was due to my talents. If I wanted to spend time with my mother, the theater was where I needed to be.

I had already made my first onstage debut at a local college when I was five years old. A man in the play with me sang "Thank Heaven for Little Girls," and at the end of the song, he kissed me on the cheek. Since I wasn't expecting it, I smacked him in front of everyone. The audience thought it was planned and laughed!

That year, I also entered the talent competition at a campground where we were vacationing. I decided to sing the inspirational song "Tomorrow" from the movie Annie. Even at a young age, I enjoyed putting a smile on others' faces and wanted to encourage them to keep hope alive. At one point during my performance, the host of the event tried to sing along with me because I had paused. He thought I had forgotten the words, but I hadn't. So I put my hands on my hips and politely said to him, "Excuse me, this is my song." Everyone thought it was hysterical, and I won second place.

Then, at age seven, I performed at a dance recital. Just before I went on stage, I told my teacher, "I've been waiting for this moment all of my life!" I still have a photo from the performance. In it, all the other kids seem confused and are looking to the right at the teacher to see what to do. Meanwhile, I am looking straight ahead at the audience, arms in the air, with a big smile on my face. I was always filled with such joy whenever I got to perform. To say that I'm naturally dramatic is an understatement.

My entrepreneurial spirit also kicked in at a young age. By the time I was ten years old, I had started my own theater company called "Starlite Productions." Friends and family members auditioned for roles, and then I had them sign a contract. I hadn't precisely mastered spelling yet, and included in the agreement was a line asking for a parent or "garden" to sign. We put on our shows at St. Mary's Parish Hall, and people donated food for us to sell. We also sold tickets, and then I divided the profit among the performers.

My mom was supportive of me being a producer and budding actress. She was a classic stage mom, and we connected through the arts. Honestly, it seemed the only way for me to reach her. She also sent me to Manhattan to take lessons with teachers who taught many famous singers and actors of the time.

I was not afraid of hard work, and many of the vocal exercises were strenuous. On occasion, I was tasked with holding heavy weights in each hand and other times pushing against the wall with all my might as I belted out three octaves.

During my high school years, I sang in Manhattan at various places, appeared on a jazz show on local TV, and performed in several plays with my mother's theater company. Film, television, and national modeling jobs followed. I will share more on that in a later chapter, but I think it's important to note that things don't usually happen overnight. Often, hard work, perseverance, tons of learning, and tons of failing occur before success. And I certainly experienced failures and heartbreaking moments of identity loss along the way.

Due to the stress at home, acting also became a place where I could hide behind the characters and live vicariously through them. Since I didn't know who I was anymore, it was easier to pretend I was someone else. So I spent several years throwing myself wholly into different roles, and acting became my primary coping mechanism. By immersing myself in the scripted life of someone else, I didn't have to face the pain of not knowing who I was or where I was headed.

One of my favorite roles to play was the ingénue, the innocent one that seemed to have it all together. I loved to pretend that life was perfect because mine was such a mess.

Not all the roles I played were lovely characters, though. When I was fourteen years old, I remember studying a dark, complex one for an audition. The character took several pills in an attempt to kill herself. For some reason, I was attracted to this role and related to elements in her thoughts, as I felt a similar darkness within. Questions like, *What is there to live for? What's the meaning of life? Why am I here? Does anyone even care? Does anyone even see me?* Resonated with me. I felt sure no one cared whether I lived or died and wasn't sure I even cared. Now I know those were lies that the devil likes to use against us, but at the time, I believed them.

Since my parents were also trying to escape their pain, they were sometimes unavailable to me for days at a time. I remember thinking, *I'm still here. I know you lost your daughter, but did you forget you still have one? Don't you see me? Don't you love me?* I often felt invisible.

Then one day, I asked my mom to take me to the mall to get something I thought I needed. When she refused, it was the last straw for me—just one more example of how she wasn't there for me unless I was doing something for her. Brimming with rage, I started yelling at her. In return, she pulled me harshly by the hair and said terrible things. My spirit crumbled, and all my anger deflated as I ran into my room.

Without much thought or any premeditation, I felt like I had become that suicidal character I had recently played. The idea of ending my life raced through my head with thoughts like, *If my mother doesn't love me and won't do what I want, then I'll get back at her by taking away the only child she has left. She doesn't see me anyway, and no one cares.*

After this justification, I decided to copy what my character did in the script, without a warning to the world, and without realizing what I was doing. I felt worthless, unwanted, and no good, and believed everyone else felt that way about me too. After I washed those pills down with water, I went to bed thinking, *I'll just never wake up.*

I ended up sleeping for about fifteen hours, and because it was a weekend, no one even noticed. But when I did wake up, I thanked God! Though I felt dizzy, confused, and half-alive, a desire to live ignited within me. Feeling terrified, I thought, *What am I doing? What did I do? I could have died,* and I went to my mom and confessed what had happened. She rushed me to the emergency room, where they gave me an IV and monitored me.

Oh, how I wish I knew then that those lies I had believed about being worthless were not true. I wish I had known that I was made for more, and that God did have a plan for my life even if I couldn't see it at the time.

We all have moments where we aren't seeing clearly and don't understand God's love and purpose for us. Have you ever felt lost and invisible, as if you couldn't go on? In these moments, it's important that we turn to the Truth and hear what God has to say. We can open our hearts and ask the questions, "Lord, do you love me? Lord, do you see me? Lord, do you have a plan for my life?" And hear Him say, "I am here, and I am near. No darkness and nothing you've ever done can keep me from you. Nothing can keep me from loving you. Nothing can keep me from living in you when you turn your life to me and invite me in. Come follow me, and I will tell you who you are. Come follow me, and I will restore your hope. Come follow me, and I will give you a future. You are not dead or half-dead, but alive, fully alive."

"The glory of God is the human person fully alive."
—*St. Irenaeus*

 PICKING UP THE PIECES

Have you ever felt like you have no idea who you are, where you are going, or how things could ever get better? Have you ever wondered, Does anyone see me? Do I really exist? How have you bought into the devil's lies?

PRAYER

Lord Jesus, I choose to open my heart to receive your love and truth. Please heal my mind, heart, body, and soul in any way that is needed. By your grace, may I always value my life and the lives of others. Please forgive me for the times that I haven't. Please help me to trust and believe in your plan for my life. Please help me to stop hiding behind things and start living fully alive as the person you created me to be. Please fill me with hope and truth and restore my life's purpose. Amen.

CHAPTER 6

FEAR AND SHAME

No foul language should come out of your mouths,
but only such as is good for needed edification,
that it may impart grace to those who hear.
—Ephesians 4:29

With a newfound desire to live, I longed to find more ways to cope with my pain. Along with acting, friendships were a huge refuge for me. Having lost my sister, I desired deep relationships and the feeling of sisterhood. Luckily, I made some fantastic friends. In fact, I still talk to my best friend, whom I met in elementary school, several times a week and adore her.

Since girlfriends were always so important to me, I cherished nights away at their houses to escape being at home. I could put my past on the shelf and just enjoy some "normal" time for a while.

To them, I appeared fun, fearless, and always up for a challenge. And I became very good at hiding my pain and deflecting it.

At the end of eighth grade, I was at a friend's house for a girls' night sleepover. She had a beautiful home with a circular driveway in front. Each room looked like it had leapt off the page of a magazine. We spent the night doing manicures and putting on makeup. Then, we tried on different dresses, did fashion shows, and took pictures. She had more clothes than anyone I knew, and one of the outfits I wore was a fitted black dress with colorful buttons around the neckline. I felt special in it and was happy she allowed me to borrow it. We were having so much fun and decided to make videos of us dancing and singing. Next, we came up with a silly idea to make a video for the boys we liked. Never in a million years did we plan to give it to them.

As part of the fashion show, I tried on a two-piece swimsuit, then was lying on the bed with my hand under my head. I said, "Is it on?" referring to the video camera, but it sounded like I said "John," the name of the boy I liked. In another part of the video, I was in between outfits in undergarments and danced around for a couple of short seconds. As young girls, we thought it was hilarious, and after we were done, I jokingly wrote "To John" on the case cover. Back home, I put it in my top dresser drawer and soon forgot all about it.

My mom was often out with her theater friends, and my dad was a workaholic, so I frequently had friends over unsupervised. At one point, someone I knew came over to visit and started snooping around. He found the "To John" video and took it!

John was going to be a senior the following year and played football at the local high school. The mischief maker decided immediately to show the video to the entire team who had gathered at another friend's house.

You can imagine how my stomach dropped when I got the phone call that he had stolen the video and they had all just watched it. I threw myself onto my bed and sobbed, feeling powerless and worried about how it would be perceived. Fortunately, a friend of mine who was there took the video and threw it away. But stories can quickly get out of hand—especially in such a small town.

By the time I started ninth grade, many rumors were spreading about me. The guys were nice as they knew the truth about the video, but the senior girls were very mean. One in particular was quite cruel because she also had a crush on John, and as it turned out, he liked me too. I was a virgin, but the girls viewed me as a threat and said terrible things insinuating that I slept around. I was often told to "watch out" because so-and-so is "on the warpath, and she wants to beat you up."

Walking through the halls my freshman year, I was always looking over my shoulder. I was a tough girl but at the same time felt targeted and feared someone might harm me. It was a terrible feeling, but I had no idea that this was bullying, and that jealousy was fueling it. I just knew that there were girls who hated me and they were spinning terrible lies.

Looking back, it's interesting how it seemed like I had everything going for me on the outside. In sixth grade, I was elected class president, beating out top male athletes who ran against me. Then I was school secretary in eighth grade. I was also part of the honor society and cast as the lead in all the school plays. People always told me how fun I was and how they loved my sense of adventure. I was known for hosting amazing house parties with tons of friends. Yet, despite all of that, I still often felt isolated and unliked by some of the older girls.

I felt so ashamed, and when I heard what they said about me, it confused me about who I really was. Each comment chipped away at my identity and distorted the view I had of myself. It hurt so much that I began to keep a very tight circle of friends and didn't trust many girls to be part of it. Consequently, I'm sure I hurt some people along the way and acted like I was too good for them. I probably appeared overly confident and unapproachable at times, and I apologize to anyone I ever hurt out of my woundedness. Now I can see that I put up walls in hopes of protecting my own heart.

It's interesting that in my ministry, I now meet several people who suffer from the idolatry of popularity. They weren't popular in school, and it had a lasting effect on them. Many felt like something was wrong with them or that they didn't belong. They are relieved when I tell them how overrated it was and how I often felt the same way. Being popular wasn't fun. It was like everything I did was under a microscope and my actions became the hot news. It was also exhausting and very lonely—just another image that I had to keep up.

When so many people seem against us and say terrible things, it's difficult to remember that God is with us. He knows our hearts and the truth. And although what others say can sting and stick to our hearts, God wants us to turn to Him to see who we really are. He knows we mess up and aren't perfect. But He loves us unconditionally and is always waiting for us to return to His love. He's with us when others betray us and helps us forgive when they cause us pain.

I don't think the person who took the video from my home realized the ripple effect his actions would create and how much it would hurt me throughout the years. While I shouldn't have made it to begin with, I thank God that He is merciful and has the power to make us new. When we surrender our lives to Him and repent, He forgives and forgets.

We need to remember that the enemy will jump at every opportunity to tear us down and try to take away our dignity and worth. However, God is greater and always wins when we give our wounds to Him. He loves us and always sees the good in us.

We should also be careful not to judge others. Only God knows the intentions in our hearts and why we do what we do. It's easy to look at the speck in someone else's eye when there is a plank in our own, and none of us are without sin. We are all struggling in some way or another. The difference is that when we surrender our lives to Christ, and He becomes the Master of our pieces, He knows how everything fits together. He knows our true beauty and what our hearts are longing for. When we judge others, we put ourselves in a dangerous place.

"For as you judge, so you will be judged, and the measure with which you measure will be measured out to you."
—*Matthew 7:2*

Nothing we have ever done is beyond the mercy of God, and He is constantly waiting for us to turn to Him. He wants us to talk to Him about our heart's desires and all of our pain. He wants to heal us so we can live in communion with one another. We can't do that when we point the finger at someone else or at ourselves, living in shame and guilt.

God desires us to come to Him to be made new and to use our bodies and beauty to bring people to Him. When we are rooted in our identity as children of God, His light shines from within and attracts others to their own encounters with Him.

We all want to be seen and known, but often we go about it the wrong way. Jesus shows us the way and offers us new life and new beginnings. He wants us to release the pain of our past to Him so He can flood us with His love.

♡ PICKING UP THE PIECES

Have you ever done something you regret and wish you could take it back? Has anyone ever bullied you? Have you ever bullied someone else because of your own insecurities? Have you ever joined in on the laughter when someone was being torn down? Think about the hurtful things others have said about you that have stuck to your heart. Surrender them to Jesus, who knows your pain and the truth about you. Even if you did something wrong, know that He is a God of mercy and forgiveness. He loves you. You are only defined by who God says you are—His beloved child in whom He is well pleased. Run into His arms and be set free!

PRAYER

Lord Jesus, I forgive others for anything negative that has ever been said about me or has been done to me. I ask you to fill me with your truth and help me to see myself as you see me. I love you and thank you. Amen.

CHAPTER 7

FINDING PURPOSE

As each one has received a gift, use it to serve one another
as good stewards of God's varied grace.
—1 Peter 4:10

Growing up, I lived in a small town, so there was no such thing as a secret. Everyone knew everything about everyone, or at least believed the rumors they heard. And the phones would be ringing off the hooks with the latest gossip. Of course, my entire family heard about what had happened with the video. So, I wanted to get out of town for a while to escape it all.

I was extremely fortunate that my loving aunts and uncles generously took me with them on vacations often. That year I was delighted to go to Arizona, where my grandparents had a second home. While there, my grandma and her friend decided to take me with them on a senior citizens' trip to Mexico. It was a long and boring bus ride, so I was ready to party when we arrived at 8:00 p.m.

My grandma, however, wanted to go to bed early. Consequently, I went on the balcony, saw some guys below in the parking lot, and decided to practice my Spanish. We were all laughing and having a good time as I yelled down to them. This went on for about ten minutes. But my grandma got angry and pulled me back inside because she wanted me to go to bed. I still wasn't tired, so I waited for her to fall asleep and then decided to sneak back out.

The guys were gone, but my grandma's friend was in the room next door, so I jumped over the balcony and knocked on her window. She was fun and lively for her age, and I knew she would still be awake.

The two of us went upstairs to the bar where other senior citizens were hanging out. Then, I immediately spotted a piano in the corner and decided to play it. While I had taken some lessons, I didn't know how to play very well at all. Still, everyone clapped enthusiastically as I finished the song. Somehow at this moment, I had become proficient at the piano, or at least convinced myself and everyone there that I knew what I was doing.

Whenever I performed, I felt incredibly alive. While I often hid behind characters, I was beginning to realize that my gifts brought joy to others, and this gave me a sense of purpose in my life. I wish I had known then how to use the gifts God gave me for His glory. I wish I had understood that I was born into my exact family for a reason—even if I didn't appreciate it at the time.

Now I see it was no mistake that my mom owned a theater company and introduced me at such an early age to the stage, which became my home. I had burning desires in my heart to bring happiness to others and elevate their spirits. The passion inside of us is something that no one could ever take away. It only grows with time and brings deep peace and exhilaration when we use it for good.

After playing the piano and feeling the room's energy, I decided to get up on the table and started to sing. I was halfway through "New York, New York" when my grandma frantically came running in to find me. She had woken up and realized I wasn't in the room and was terrified. Wearing her nightgown and with big, fuzzy curlers in her hair, she yelled at me and quickly dragged me out of the bar—to the shock and laughter of all the people watching. As we made our way out of the room, my grandmother's friend and I looked at each other and tried to hide our smiles to appear more serious.

I feel bad that I worried my grandma so much. But I thank God that she always prayed for me and never gave up despite the heartache I put her through. She was my rock, a source of strength, and an example of unconditional love in my life. It was the love I so desperately needed to experience—a glimpse of how God loves us no matter what we do wrong. Whenever I experienced these moments of unbelievable affection, it made me never want to hurt anyone again.

When someone loves you, truly loves you, the desire in the heart is to reciprocate that love. Since we are made in the image of God, we are wired for deep connections and relationships. My grandma always believed in me and encouraged me to trust God even in moments of weakness.

Although I had no idea then the fullness of my life's purpose, looking back, I can see patterns that revealed my calling and brought deep peace to my soul. In those moments, I felt free and alive—like an "Aha!" moment where everything just made sense. When we use the gifts God gave us, we have a sense of belonging, and the joy that comes from being who we are created to be is contagious.

Discovery of our gifts and talents is part of the glue that the Master of our pieces uses to put us back together. Imagine what God sees when He looks at us. He knows our every mistake, but at the same time, He knows all the gifts we've been given to bring His love and goodness to others. God doesn't make mistakes. He makes Masterpieces.

Every one of us is unique, yet we are complete in Him. We have different personalities, talents, and spiritual gifts to serve the Lord and build the body of Christ.

"There are different kinds of spiritual gifts but the same Spirit, there are different forms of service but the same Lord; there are different workings but the same God who produces all of them in everyone. To each individual, the manifestation of the Spirit is given for some benefit."
—1 Corinthians 12:4–7

As we look back and review our lives, we can begin to acknowledge our gifts and see how the Lord would like to use us. Among these are gifts of wisdom, faith, healing, prophecy, discernment of spirits, tongues, and interpretation of tongues, to name a few. God doesn't give us all of them because He wants us to need Him and one another.

The enemy will often try to get us to focus on flaws in others and ourselves. While none of us is perfect, the world would be a much different place if we could see the good in each other, ourselves, and the gifts within.

Where and how we become alive is an indicator of our life's purpose. And while mine isn't to stand on tables and sing "New York, New York," singing, speaking, acting, and entertaining people are undoubtedly a part of it.

I spent many years using these gifts in the wrong direction with films, plays, songs, and ads that didn't glorify God. But when we learn to redirect our passions for His purpose, it's like a beautiful flower begins to open up. I now realize my deepest desire is to lift people up to the truth of God's plans for them through the arts and media. God reveals all in His timing. We just need to be open to hearing Him and believing in His plan for us.

For our gifts to bear good fruit, we must remain in Him and have a deep relationship with Him.

"Remain in me, as I remain in you. Just as a branch cannot bear fruit on its own unless it remains on the vine, so neither can you unless you remain in me. I am the vine, you are the branches. Whoever remains in me and I in him will bear much fruit, because without me you can do nothing."
—John 15:4–5

With God, all things are possible. He wants to lavish gifts on us, not take them away. Then, He wants us to use the gifts He has given us to bring Him glory and lead others to Him. We don't need to understand everything or try to figure it all out. We just need to say "yes" and direct our will to His.

I know many people who have gifts that I lack, and I appreciate them very much. For example, I don't have the gift of administration and would make a terrible secretary. I'm sure everyone's meetings would be all mixed up if I oversaw scheduling them. My spreadsheets don't even print out on the same page like they are supposed to. If I tried to do that job, others would get mad at me, and I wouldn't be productive. However, the world doesn't go around without someone who has been graced with these gifts—we all need each other.

I often joke that I have the heart of an artist but not the hands. In my mind, I can visualize a beautiful picture I want to draw. However, when I try to put it on paper, it becomes stick figures. No one has any idea what I'm trying to portray. But someone else who has the gift of art can express this beauty so that others can perceive God and His goodness in it.

Spend some time in quiet reflection and ask the Lord to bring to mind the gifts you have and how they can be used to serve Him. Even in your home, workplace, and encounters with others, you can become a light in someone else's darkness.

 **PICKING UP THE PIECES**

What are some funny and good memories from your past that remind you who you are and reveal part of God's plan for you? What talents, gifts, and graces has He given you to share with others to bring them joy? Maybe you know how to play an instrument, or you know how to sing or draw. Perhaps you play a sport well and haven't played in years. Maybe you're a writer, and God is calling you to share your story. Whatever it is, acknowledge your gift and see how you can use it to bring God's love to others.

PRAYER

Lord Jesus, thank you for the gifts and talents you have given me. Please help me to know them and use them to bring you glory. Help me remember funny memories from my past that uncover glimpses of who I am in You. Amen.

CHAPTER 8

NEW BEGINNINGS

Do to others as you would have them do to you.
—Luke 6:31

My trip to Mexico was filled with adventure, but it's amazing how quickly good memories can fade. The pains of our past seem to linger longer, and high school is a tough time for most people. Figuring out who you are and not letting others define you isn't easy. Trying to figure out if God is real and accepting His love isn't easy either. And back then, after everything I had been through, my faith and trust in Him were nearly nonexistent.

When I was in ninth grade, my family decided to send me on a Catholic teen retreat. I complained and whined the entire car ride there because I felt so far away from God and didn't want to go. On top of that, I was at the age when I wanted to do the exact opposite of anything my parents asked me to do.

The retreat center was tucked away deep in the woods on several acres of land. As we arrived, I noticed a peace and tranquility radiating from the grounds, which was something foreign to me.

When I went inside, I didn't know anyone else except one of my cousins who had also been forced to go. Growing up, she and I would often make up games and pretend to be detectives. We walked around the neighborhood looking for things that seemed out of place and would look at each other with one eyebrow up and say in a sing-song voice, "That's another mystery." Even at a young age, I was intrigued by the mystery of life, craved to understand it, and enjoyed discovering it.

In my faith now, it's exciting to enter into the mystery of God. There's always something new to be found, like the unfathomable depths of His love and the deep intimacy that I always wanted. Not knowing what I will find around each turn is exciting, and on some days, I see God everywhere. But in my past, I was so blind as I was barely searching and couldn't see a thing.

I also longed for my cousin to be like a sister to me; however, no one could ever replace Maria and an emptiness remained within. At the retreat, I remember being in the bathroom, getting ready for bed the first evening, and feeling envious of those that had their sisters with them. They shared hair accessories and clothes, and it was obvious that they had deep relationships with each other. They were so comfortable together, and I watched them laugh and joke around. I often felt like an outcast around others that had siblings because it was a constant reminder of having lost my only one. I felt left behind. And in my mind, God was mean for allowing this to happen to my family and me.

As the retreat went on, I eventually began to let my guard down and was amazed when it turned out to be a wonderful experience. I made friends as the days progressed, and the music and talks were inspiring.

Inside, I fervently longed for truth and love but was unsure how to receive it. At bedtime, they told us that the chapel would be open all night long if we wanted to pray. When I woke up around midnight, I couldn't fall back asleep. A deep yearning was welling up inside to go, but I didn't feel worthy and questioned whether I should. However, it was as if I couldn't stay away any longer—I was being called—so I went.

I didn't understand that the Holy Spirit lived in me and was prompting me to spend some quiet time in prayer. It had been years since I had really prayed, and the world can be so loud. That night, for the first time in a long time, I had the chance to have a real heart-to-heart talk with God—minutes passed into hours. Somehow, I was aware of being in His presence, that He was real, and that He loved me. I also became aware of just how far I had strayed from Him.

On my knees, I was praying and weeping, hunched over in a fetal position. As I began releasing all my pain, sorrow, and shame to Him, I felt as if I was being renewed. Soon, other teens began to enter the room, and the sight of my peers also being called there in the middle of the night was very moving.

Additionally, the damage that gossip had caused in my life came to mind during my prayer. Reflecting on how much it had hurt, I didn't want others to experience what I had felt and resolved never to inflict such pain on someone else. It also came to light how I tended to pull away from relationships. So when I returned from the retreat, I tried to be more open and let people come into my life. I wanted to be friends with everyone, and I didn't want anyone to feel left out. I felt called to stick up for people—especially if I thought there was an injustice.

Suddenly, I also remembered elementary school when I had noticed that there were different groups and cliques on the playground. Some were into sports, some into art, others into science, and others just thought they were too cool for everyone else. However, I was never super "cliquey" and didn't feel like I belonged to any one of these groups. Instead, I created my own, and people from each group came to be a part of it, which was beautiful.

In Christ, we are all one and called to love one another. I didn't realize at such a young age that God was calling me to evangelism. Sadly, we can be born with gifts and turn away from them because of our woundedness. I wish I had been able to see the blessings in others then, the way I do now. My deepest desire was to build them up, and bring them together—not to run away, hide, or put myself on a pedestal. I was thankful for the Lord's light and the reminder of my purpose during this time with Him.

Then, toward the end of the retreat, the leaders surprised us with letters from our loved ones. Many of my family members wrote to me, and their words of kindness pierced my heart like never before and brought healing. I'd had no idea how they felt about me. Words of truth can eradicate the lies in our hearts and tear down the walls. If only we would spend more time speaking words of love that raise each other up!

Coming back from the retreat, I felt changed and made new and hoped it would last. I was aware that something extraordinary had happened in the chapel that night. But I didn't know exactly what that encounter was all about. Too quickly, though, within a couple of weeks, I got caught up in sin and distractions. I began to fall once again into all the things of the world and more vanities, just like in the parable of the sower.

"And he spoke to them at length in parables, saying: 'A sower went out to sow. And as he sowed, some seed fell on the path, and birds came and ate it up. Some fell on rocky ground, where it had little soil. It sprang up at once because the soil was not deep, and when the sun rose it was scorched, and it withered for lack of roots. Some seed fell among thorns, and the thorns grew up and choked it. But some seed fell on rich soil, and produced fruit, a hundred or sixty or thirtyfold. Whoever has ears ought to hear.'"
—*Matthew 13:3–9*

Indeed, I lacked roots because I wasn't living in my identity as a beloved daughter of God. I also didn't have a community of other teens practicing the faith journey alongside me. And I was still very selfish and immature in many ways. However, after this retreat, I always tried to remember to stand up for others and to not leave anyone out. It was a grace I received that has remained. People who knew me understood that I had their back and would fight for them in any situation that seemed unjust.

And although I couldn't admit it at the time, I was grateful my parents persisted and made me go on that retreat. It was a wonderful gift, and my heart glimpsed what it was like to be filled with love and mercy for others.

My experience brings to mind the prodigal son's story and how God is always waiting for our return. We think we know what we are doing and try to go at it alone. Then, once we've exhausted all our resources, we realize that nothing satisfies us and there is nowhere to go but back to Him. Although we feel unworthy, He's so happy with our homecoming that He wants to embrace us and throw a big party. That's one of the most surprising things about God—His love is constant and never fails. He never stops looking for us when we're lost, and He always wants to re-establish our identity. Our authority over the lies in the world and the lies in our hearts is in Him. He IS the Truth. We need to read the Bible and know His Word if we want to see the truth of who we are.

"Indeed, the word of God is living and effective, sharper than any two-edged sword, penetrating even between soul and spirit, joints and marrow, and able to discern reflections and thoughts of the heart."
—Hebrews 4:12

In His Word, we discover that we are loved, chosen, forgiven, healed, redeemed, and created for a purpose. Once we believe we are who He says we are and He is who He says He is, we will find our true joy. We will need to make adjustments in our lives but will remain in pain and misery without these changes. While I didn't stay rooted in Christ long after the retreat, years later, I would finally return home to Him.

 PICKING UP THE PIECES

What is your earliest experience of God that you can remember?

When was a time that you felt His presence or felt renewed? What

changes did you make in your life after that? How long did it last?

Did you keep up your prayer and relationship with God?

PRAYER

Lord Jesus, help me to be kind and loving to everyone in my life. Please help me to not leave others out and to be more inviting to them. Please help me encounter you and be on fire for the things that you are on fire for. May my heart remain on fire and never burn out. Amen.

CHAPTER 9

WORTHLESSNESS AND UNWORTHINESS

Death and life are in the power of the tongue;
those who choose one shall eat its fruit.
—Proverbs 18:21

After the retreat, I continued to chase worldly pursuits in hopes of getting that euphoric feeling back. While my friendships were fulfilling, they weren't enough to satisfy my longing for love. My search for love and a boyfriend absorbed me and helped distract from the pain in my life.

I still have my diary from when I was eleven years old, and it's hilarious for me to look back on the things I wrote, such as: *Oh, I'm so in love with Greg. He's the one! He's amazing! Then, a month later, I would write, Now Richie is my boyfriend. He's the best, and we're madly in love! Joelle and Richie married forever! Two months later, I would say, I'm in love with Michael, and I've never met anyone like him before!*

At age eleven, these were sweet, innocent crushes, but they revealed the desire in my heart to love and be loved. However, at the time, I had no idea what love even was because I was constantly running away from Love Himself.

When I was in middle and high school, the hot topics among the girls in my grade were, "Who do you like? Who's your date for prom?" So by tenth grade, I thought I needed a boyfriend. But after the unhealed wounds from freshman year, I decided not to date anyone from my school because I didn't want everyone to have a play-by-play of my relationships.

Finally, I met a guy from another town. I did have feelings for him, but sadly, he became more of an object to me than a person I truly loved. I was trying to fill a void—one he would never be able to fill. We dated for a while, but the problem was that I with him for the wrong reasons. This guy was not good for me and deep down I knew it. I often wanted to break up with him but had many fears about letting the relationship go.

He would sing a song to me called "Can't Find a Better Man" and tell me that I would never find anyone better. He may have thought he was joking, but when you hear someone say this repeatedly to you, it gets confusing. I felt stuck and unworthy.

He was very handsome, with olive skin, jet-black hair, and bright blue eyes. But he was obsessed with his appearance and spent several hours a day at the gym. I can still envision him looking at himself in the mirror and flexing his muscles. Quite honestly, it was such a turnoff to me.

In my heart, I knew I didn't want to marry this guy and that there must be a better man out there, because what kind of man would tell me otherwise? Deep down I knew it wasn't true. But I didn't want to be without a boyfriend, as I felt it would make me more vulnerable.

I didn't want to lose the safety of having someone to take me to the prom or be by my side on a Friday night. So I kept him as a boyfriend for all the wrong reasons and held onto him until someone else came along. I was lost at the time and had no idea how deeply God wanted to restore me and redeem my shame.

I was always looking for the True One but was looking for love in all the wrong places. I was looking for love in a human being when The One I really needed was already within me. The True One didn't tell me that I couldn't do better, or that I wasn't made for more, or that I had to be tied to bad relationships just to have someone in my life. Of course, it wasn't until several years later that I learned Jesus is The One and is the hero that I sang about in my songwriting.

In college, I wrote and recorded a song called "Save My Heart." The chorus said, "Save my heart, I almost gave up on love. Come be my hero; it's you I love." Looking back, I realize I was searching for someone to save my heart. I fervently wanted someone to speak truth into it.

Ironically, I recently found videos of me singing in my college dorm room, and on the wall behind me hangs a huge picture of Jesus. Of course, my grandma always gave me statues of the Blessed Mother and tons of images of the Lord to hang and display. Although I was far from Him, it's as if He was always behind me, just waiting for me to turn around.

I didn't know then that there is freedom in solitude rather than being with the wrong person, as I didn't have Jesus in my life the way I do now. The culture told me I needed to have a boyfriend and somebody by my side, so that's what I sought.

The relationship was certainly one of convenience, and when I ended it with him for someone else, he didn't take it so well. I'll never forget being in college in New York City right after breaking up. He found a way to get past the security guards in the lobby and up the elevator. Then he got a student to let him in on my floor since you needed a key to access it.

I was in the communal hallway bathroom in the toilet stall. I had just locked the door when suddenly, it started shaking and someone was yelling at me. Then, I saw an eyeball looking through the crack, like something out of a horror film. Trembling with fear, I thought, *Who is looking at me through the bathroom stall? Who is screaming at me and accusing me of crazy things?* Eventually, I recognized it was my ex's voice and realized I had to face him in person. However, I was finally learning to rise up. I decided to tell him, "You know what? I can find a better man, and you can't speak to me like that anymore. You lost the best thing that you ever had."

While I'm glad I stood up for myself, I also acknowledge that it was wrong that I used him. My fear of being alone was bigger than my heart, and I stayed in the relationship for the wrong reasons. Sadly, we both hurt each other.

Why do relationships at times become like a god to us? Why would we rather be with someone who's not good for us than wait for the Lord to send us the one who is? It wasn't until several years later, when my heart was finally open, that I did find "The One." His name is Jesus. May we never give up and never let anyone else define us. We are made worthy in Him, and He always has the best plan for our lives. We just need to trust Him more.

 PICKING UP THE PIECES

Have you stayed in a bad relationship just to have someone by your side? Has anyone ever said something to you that made you feel like you couldn't leave a relationship? Are you afraid of being alone? Are there any relationships you need to surrender to God? Is there anyone from your past that you thought of as you read this chapter that you need to forgive, pray for, or let go of?

PRAYER

Lord Jesus, please forgive me for any time that I have used another as an object and didn't see them as a person. Please guide my relationships and put people in my life who will value me and love me for who I am. Help me to know that you live in me and that I am eternally loved. Amen.

CHAPTER 10

BETRAYAL

*When you stand to pray, forgive anyone against whom
you have a grievance, so that your heavenly Father may in turn
forgive you your transgressions.*
—Mark 11:25

After that relationship ended, I began to explore Manhattan even more. Living there was freeing for me in many ways, and I was incredibly happy to be out of my depressing childhood home.

I was also very grateful to receive a music scholarship toward a wonderful university. It was granted for being the first person from our school in over twenty-five years to get accepted into a state choir. For the competition, I sang opera, of all things!

Additionally, a renowned concert promoter was representing me, and I performed at various well-known venues in New York City. And at one point, I met with a famous singer's manager who told me that to make it in the music business, I had to write my own songs. Honestly, I had no idea what I was doing but started writing and spending a lot of time in the recording studio. Then, one of my songs ended up in a film, and I was later asked to do an international tour with a performance group. However, I decided to study abroad in Italy instead.

It seemed like I had it all and was living the high life, as I had friends that were very successful and prominent. I was invited to dinner with a billionaire's group a couple of times, and the person throwing the events later became a US President. I would go to elite parties at a socialite's penthouse and be seated next to several celebrities. And I got to go backstage at many concerts to meet the singers and bands. On one occasion, a group invited me to dinner with a famous Italian singer, but I was being snobby and said I was too busy to go. I was becoming so used to being in that scene that nothing was a big deal to me anymore. Of course, now I would love to meet him as his songs touch my heart, and I admire the gift that God has given him.

One friend I met at the socialite's penthouse had his own limousine, and I would have the driver drop him home after we went to dinner. Then he took me to pick up my friends. Picture a bunch of college girls driving all over Manhattan hanging out of the sunroof and windows!

However, this lifestyle also had a dark side. That same man, who was much older than me, tried to impress me by taking me to luxury stores and buying me several dresses and shoes. The bill totaled thousands and thousands of dollars, which should have been a warning sign to me—because not long after, he offered to pay me $10 million to be his girlfriend! As a young and lost soul, I can't say that I didn't think about it, but by the grace of God, I told him that I couldn't. I was repulsed by the idea and couldn't even bring myself to kiss him—no amount of money can buy love. After my reversion back to the faith, I donated the extravagant dresses he bought me to a friend's daughter. It was very liberating to let them go and not care about the things of the world anymore.

I also went out with a well-known celebrity, and after a couple of dates, I realized he was selfish and only interested in one thing. He often played dreamy leading-man roles, and I was disappointed that he wasn't as charming in real life as he was in films and on television.

I experienced disillusionment, because I was looking for a leader—a true man who saw me for me. I desperately wanted to feel loved and valued, but the relationship was superficial, and the allure of his looks quickly wore off. I didn't have an emotional attraction to him either or feel like we had much in common. Then, after he tried to pressure me into doing something I didn't want to do, I told him the relationship was finished. He appeared shocked that I wasn't interested and attempted to persuade me to stay. He said he wanted us to have a good day together and go shopping after lunch, and that he didn't want me to leave. However, a simple "I'm sorry" would have gotten him much further. I told him I never wanted to see him again, left, and didn't look back.

Dissatisfied with the fancy parties, stars, and nightlife, I continued to crave deep friendships—which weren't easy to find. I had one friend in particular I thought I could trust because we had traveled together and had such a great time. One night, she asked me to go out to a club, and since I loved dressing up and dancing, I agreed.

She knew a guy who was good friends with a well-known Catholic celebrity, who was actually very kind to me. I always wondered why I met him not once but twice. Only God could see that years later we would end up serving the Lord together in an interview for a Catholic film he produced and starred in.

I went out with my friend and this group a second time in New York City, where we met up with another star. This man, a household name on every continent, whispered to someone else that he wanted me to go home with him that night. When the message got to me, I thought it sounded crazy. I said, "I haven't even spoken to him, and he doesn't even know me." His friend replied, "Well, yeah, just so you know, he has a contest going on, and he's up to two thousand women right now because girls don't say no to him." I said, "Well, then, let me be one of the first." I told his friend to tell him, "No way. I'm not interested. No, thank you!" I thank God that I didn't go home with this guy just to be part of his game and one of his objects of use. Power can get to a person's head, and thankfully, I resisted his attempt.

The girl who had invited me out that night did have a fun group of friends, though, and I went out with her again a few weeks later to another club. However, this night was much different. The huge venue had a bar downstairs and several lounge areas upstairs. It was so dark that it was hard to see, and the place was packed with people, leaving little standing room.

At the bar, someone my friend knew ordered us strong drinks. I should have watched the bartender make them and been more aware and less trusting of the people around me, because it didn't take long before I felt tipsy. Soon, the room began spinning as someone must have slipped a drug into my drink, and I ended up collapsing on the floor.

My grandma, who always kept me updated on the news, had been warning me that these things were regularly happening to several unsuspecting girls. However, I was naïve and never thought it would happen to me. This was one of many times in my life that I wish I had listened to her and taken what she said more seriously.

There I was, upstairs in a corner on the floor near a black couch, unable to move because I had lost all my motor skills, couldn't walk, and could barely speak. Easily, someone could have taken advantage of me, and no one would have even noticed. I was there for hours, hoping no one would hurt me, and used all the strength I had to try to say the word "home." Finally, my friend found me. She had been busy flirting with guys all night and hadn't even noticed I was in trouble.

She was having too much fun to leave, but I couldn't walk, so she asked one of her friends to carry me out in his arms. Tall and muscular, he walked away looking like a "knight in shining armor" as he hailed a cab to bring me home. When we arrived at my apartment building, this stranger carried me through the lobby past a security guard. I was completely incapacitated, but nobody intervened.

He brought me to my room, and other than being placed in my bed, I have no recollection of anything that happened after that. The next morning when I woke up, I wasn't wearing the outfit I'd worn to the club. Instead, I was dressed in my silky, pink, pinstriped pajamas—having no idea how they got on me. Having taken this event to prayer and after discussing it with a counselor, I don't believe I was raped that night. I was told that if such an experience happens, parts of the incident are usually retained by the body or mind as traumatic memories.

Regardless, I felt violated simply by the thought that somebody had changed me out of my clothes. Maybe he thought he was doing a good deed, but why didn't he just bring me home and leave? Waking up, a series of questions raced through my head. *What if he did do something else to me that I just don't remember? How could my friend not make sure to get me home safely? How could she just send me home with a stranger?* I didn't even know the guy's name and didn't have his phone number. There was no way for me to follow up.

For years, that event haunted me. I repeatedly wondered, *How did I get into my pajamas? What did he see? What did he do to me? And what kind of friend would leave me like that?*

The next day, I felt extremely sick, so I only had a brief conversation with her expressing my hurt and anger that she hadn't seen me home safely. While I realize that I shouldn't have been living such a party life and should have been more aware of my surroundings, her selfishness had gotten in the way that night and put me at risk.

We're called to help others, love them, and desire their good. I have chosen to forgive her, as Jesus shows us the way to life is to forgive and be forgiven. It's not easy, but it's the choice that sets us free. My friend and I never reconciled because I lost contact with her, but holding onto the offense only caused me pain. Letting it go allowed me to eventually build deep relationships with others.

The enemy loves when we hold grudges and don't forgive because it's an open door for him to keep us in the hurts of our past. In ministry, I encounter so many people who say what happened to them is unforgivable or that they are unable to forgive. While the offense may be terrible, we have the choice to transfer it to God for His justice.

Unforgiveness can make our minds become like a gerbil wheel as we relive the pain over and over again. We need to make a simple act of the will and say, "Jesus, this happened, but I choose to forgive and transfer the offense to you to deal with." This sets us free and releases the pain to Him.

Each of us will be held accountable for everything we say and do. Since we are made in the image of God and God is love, an offense against love is an offense against God. It will be so painful for any of us to see how much we missed the mark.

We are all prone to selfishness, and it's only through a relationship with Christ that we begin to become more like Him. We can learn to love—even if it means denying our desires for the good of another. Let us ask God to give us the grace and strength not to turn inward but to turn outward. When someone needs help, let us be their help. Let us not turn our back on those in need, and let us beg God for healthy relationships and good people to come into our lives. People who help restore our identity, not take it away. And may we forgive all those that have hurt us whether they meant to or not.

 PICKING UP THE PIECES

Has someone been selfish and put their needs ahead of yours, to the point of compromising you and possibly harming you? Have you ever done that to someone else? Do you need to forgive someone who once violated you? Are you ready to surrender the hurt to God?

PRAYER

Lord Jesus, please help me to not be selfish and to be available to help others. Would you please grace me with friends that I can trust and who desire my good? I freely choose to forgive others for the times they were selfish and hurt me. By your grace, I forgive anyone who has ever violated me and know that justice is yours. I surrender the situation to you. Amen.

MOMENT OF TRUTH

Amen, I say to you, whatever you bind on earth
shall be bound in heaven, and whatever you loose
on earth shall be loosed in heaven.
—Matthew 18:18

I continued to hide my pain in life behind more accomplishments, successes, and characters and began to pull away from God even more. Consumed by materialism, I was seeking to find my identity in the world. I wanted to be redeemed and saved but honestly had no idea how to go about doing that. As I looked for value and worth in all the wrong places, my life became characterized by checking more boxes that I thought would make me happy. However, each one left me emptier than the last.

It got to the point where I wanted to run away from everything, and I thought maybe moving to another country would fix things. Since I was minoring in Italian in college, I took the opportunity to study abroad and lived in Siena, Italy, and then Florence. My grandparents were originally from a small town near Naples, and when I was younger, they spoke in Italian to tell secrets so the kids wouldn't understand. So now, I wanted to get back at them and learn the language. No one knew me in Italy, and I thought moving there would provide a fresh start and I could just be me.

I desired to be loved for who I was rather than for what I could do for someone else or who I could introduce them to. The problem was, I didn't know how to start over and found myself doing things to fit in with different groups. Sadly, it didn't take very long for me to start making some bad choices.

There I was in, a beautiful country, taking field trips to holy places, but I had no idea of the presence of God within and around me. I saw incorruptible bodies of saints that were miraculously preserved after death and didn't decompose. I viewed artwork by many great painters but was blind to the beauty right in front of me. The Italian gelato and pizza I ate had my attention more than the amazing, historic churches I saw.

There were many unforgettable moments, though, and I was enthralled by the culture and way of life. Everything seemed like an adventure, and I loved the sense of community and spending time together for meals.

After dinner, I would always go on walks with friends in the town square and meet up with others. The Italians call this *passeggiata*. I loved it so much and dreamed of moving there permanently one day. Many of my relatives still live in Italy, and I long to go back and visit them as well.

While there, I decided to host videos of my experiences and travels around Italy, France, Germany, Holland, and Austria. Being on camera came naturally to me, but I didn't realize then that hosting would eventually become a part of my life. I just found it an exciting thing to do. I was often surrounded by friends and then got them to participate in the videos, and we even recorded some fun skits in different cities.

It was a fantastic time, but being in another country didn't take away the deep loneliness inside as I hoped it would. I was becoming aware that the problem wasn't in the world; rather, it was within me and created conflict in my heart.

In some moments I tried to seek God and ask for His help, but they were short-lived. In Florence, I remember being one bridge over from the stunning "Ponte Vecchio"—I still smile anytime I see a picture of it. I bought a fresh turkey panini for lunch, then sat on a ledge just off the bridge. Choosing to eat in solitude, I tried to talk to God about the sadness in my heart, but I couldn't hear His response. My sin had not only blinded me but also made me deaf to His voice.

I now know that God is always talking to us in various ways and constantly trying to communicate His will. However, even if I did hear Him at that moment, I doubted that it was Him. *What would God would want to do with me anyway?* I thought, as I felt so unworthy of His love. Thus, I still struggled, and my desire for a new start in Italy didn't go as planned. I ended up partying way too much, which left me unfulfilled and feeling more lost than before I arrived.

Shortly after I returned to the US, I went to visit my family, and Grandma looked me up and down and said sternly, "You're going to Confession tonight!" I tried to put up a fight and said, "No, I'm not!" She said, "Yes, you are!" I replied, "No, I'm not!" She stared at me gravely and said, "Get in the car." Grandma was a bold Italian woman and usually got her way. I had no choice but to agree, as I secretly knew she was right. Although I hadn't shared anything with her, somehow, she knew that my soul was in a terrible state.

When we got to the church, I didn't want to go into the confessional. I was scared to confront the truth of how far I was from God and didn't even know how to verbalize it. As we stood outside the confessional door, I told her, "Grandma, no, I don't think I'm going to go in." She took me by my hair, threw me in, and slammed the door behind me. As I tumbled to the chair inside, I tried to muster up a respectable, "Hello, Father," and did my best to act cool and like everything was fine. The priest looked surprised, as he didn't know or recognize me, but he knew my grandmother and had seen her throw me in. I began to tremble while trying to look confident and in control as I held back tears as best as I could. And I pretended to be angry at her for dragging me there. However, in my heart, I knew that I desperately needed a push. It was one of the best things anyone has ever done for me, a true act of mercy.

Although I didn't understand it at the time, I received a profound grace by giving my mess to God. He was beginning to form the message. But as soon as I returned to my life in the city, I quickly fell off the path yet again.

You may have heard the phrase, "Show me your friends, and I'll show you your future." That was part of my problem. My friends were my enemies. My friends were my vanities, and they were leading me in the wrong direction. Now, that's not to say that I didn't have a couple of good friends in my life, but they were not the ones I was primarily surrounding myself with. I now know that it's essential to spend time with people running the race with us toward freedom and life in Christ. We should be challenging one another and running with everything we have. But unfortunately, I wasn't running toward Him at all. I was running away and felt ashamed, broken, and unredeemable.

Sometimes we need someone to throw us into the confessional or into a church to realize that God is with us and never leaves us. He is merciful and forgiving and wants to welcome us home no matter what we've done. Our Father's house shouldn't be somewhere we fear. We should feel comfortable and at peace there because it's exactly where we belong.

I didn't know that the priest acts *in persona Christi* (in the person of Christ) and that my Confession was a conversation and reconciliation with God Himself.

"I will give you the keys to the kingdom of heaven. Whatever you bind on earth shall be bound in heaven; and whatever you loose on earth shall be loosed in heaven."
—Matthew 16:19

I wish I'd known His merciful heart then and understood how Jesus died to save us. He forgives and forgets once we bring our sins to Him. The forgiveness of sin is a big deal, and if we don't accept that, it's as if Jesus died for no reason. The entire point is that He loves us so much that He emptied Himself out on the cross for us—to redeem, restore, and empower us to be His disciples.

The Sacrament of Reconciliation gives us the healing grace to overcome sin. However, many times, the wounds underneath the sins are hidden. We need to get to the roots to find out why we behave the way we do. In our shattered pieces are the answers, and when we bring them to God, He puts us back together. He heals the wounds of un-love in our hearts as He sees us and knows us completely. He doesn't just see the pieces; He sees the whole picture. And he knows the beauty of what can happen when we are reconciled with the truth and rejoices at our return.

Since we all have blind spots, it's essential to have people on this journey with us who are honest and tell us when we need to go to Confession—especially when we can't see it ourselves. Hopefully, we can get to the point where we seek it out independently and walk into our Father's house trusting that He wants to forgive us and welcome us home. Then, eventually, we can become the one who leads others to His mercy.

♡ PICKING UP THE PIECES

Who are you surrounding yourself with? Who is being Christ to you when you are in darkness? How can you be that person to someone else? Who do you see struggling right now that needs an extra push? Who needs the freedom to know that they are loved just as they are and that nothing they have ever done could keep God away? How can you become God's light and bring hope to others?

PRAYER

Lord Jesus, thank you for the people in our lives that lead by a good example and encourage us. Help us to run the race together toward you. Thank you for never giving up on us and for giving us a push when we need it through the hands of another. Amen.

BROKEN DREAMS

A thief comes only to steal and slaughter and destroy;
I came so that they might have life and have
it more abundantly.
—John 10:10

Despite the heartaches and dramas in my life, I loved the hustle and bustle of life in New York City. I often rode the subway, took taxicabs, and enjoyed walking around to see the cultural diversity. I also continued to audition as an actress and model, and by the grace of God, started to book more jobs.

I never actually planned on being a model; it just happened. Honestly, I didn't even think I would be good at it, and my self-esteem was not nearly as high as I projected it to be. But someone told me that I should meet with modeling agents, and I ended up signing with several.

Before I knew it and to my surprise, I was doing national ads and even landed on a billboard in Times Square. I was also a lingerie model for one of the largest retailers in the country and the cover model for many romance novels. The book covers were shot in live action and then painted. The photo shoots were extremely romantic and steamy with gorgeous leading men. I never actually read the books, so I can only imagine what "my" character was like. Now I shudder to think that people were envisioning me as that person!

The thought that these images appeared in major chain stores all over the country is so upsetting to me now, although I didn't think anything was wrong with it at the time. I was just happy to be working and couldn't see clearly because my heart was caught up in the things of the world.

Then at one point, a well-known photographer wanted me to do a test shoot, which is when the photographer does the photo shoot for free to build his portfolio. The model also gets to keep the photos for hers. It's a win-win situation, or at least it's supposed to be. This particular photographer had worked with many celebrities and models, so his portfolio was already awe-inspiring, and I was honored that he wanted to do a shoot with me.

I showed up at his multimillion-dollar penthouse, and the white carpets and sleek furniture were picturesque, but I immediately felt nervous being there alone with him. When he noticed my discomfort, he offered me alcohol, saying I needed to relax. Then, he gave me a sheer navy-blue scarf and asked me to take my top off to put it around me. I was reluctant, but he said it was true art and all the models did it. If I wanted to make it in this business, he said, I had to do it too. To me, it became a challenge, an almost do-or-die situation. But when I left that day, I felt like I walked away without a piece of myself. I felt that I had given something away, and regret began to set in.

While the shots turned out beautiful and had an old Hollywood flair to them, this uncomfortable encounter didn't sit well with me. I told a friend about it, and they suggested I ask the photographer for the film files so I could get copies made. Luckily, they weren't stored on his computer yet, and when I got them, I immediately threw them away. Later he called me to get them back, and I told him how he had made me feel and that they were gone forever. He threatened me by saying I would never work as a model again and tried to use his clout to make me fearful. But his words had no power, and I continued to book jobs anyway.

However, despite my modeling successes, my heart was always drawn more to acting. It wasn't easy, and I heard "no" many times before a "yes," which was very painful, but I didn't give up amid the rejection. I appeared in independent films, landed lead roles in plays, and even hosted a TV show. Looking back, I'm saddened by some of the parts I played, although they seemed so normal at the time because I was blinded by sin.

Whether it was skimpy and seductive clothing, inappropriate language, or being in a film about vampires, I'm heartbroken at the example I was setting in the world.

One time, I was on the set of a major horror film with a famous director. He wanted to do a close-up of my reaction to a well-known actress in the project. It took hours for the crew to capture the shot, and I was thrilled to be in a film that would be shown worldwide. However, when I went to the movie theater and found that my scene had been cut, I was mad at God. Little did I know that He was protecting me, because ironically, the film was about being cursed, and God was telling me that I was "blessed." When God closes a door, it's for a reason. He always has better things planned for us, even if we can't see it, and even if it hurts.

The distortions in the world were beyond my comprehension at the time, and it was as if I had grown immune to it all. The photo shoots, films, and content all seemed so acceptable, but much of it was a complete misuse of my talents and gifts. Even some of my song lyrics were so sensual that I can't even write them to share with you. I had become desensitized to violence, materialism, and overt sexuality like many people in our culture today. And I was a far cry from "The Sweetest Girl" award that I had won in elementary school, which is who I really wanted to be.

My career may have looked fulfilling, but I was empty inside because I wasn't bringing good into the world. I knew I wasn't satisfied, but sadly, I didn't understand why and thought the next role would be the one to fill me—of course, it never did.

At one point, I came close to booking a lead role on a major TV show that I was dying to be on and was crushed when I didn't get the part. They told me it was down to just me and another girl, and it was devastating to have made it that far and not get cast.

I have no idea how I handled all the rejection I faced in between the times when I did book things. Without realizing it, I was coping with my self-esteem issues by hiding further behind a mask of confidence. But I remember many days when I felt discouraged, exhausted, and not good enough—as if I couldn't go on. Inside me was a fire raging to express myself, but the opportunities seemed few and far between.

The "casting couch" was also a real thing. I saw more of it in Los Angeles than in New York, but it was something I could never bring myself to participate in. I auditioned for many roles that I didn't get and would later watch on TV and be surprised to see the actress who got the part. She would have a different hair color or be a different height than what I'd been told they were looking for. Then, I would learn through others that the actress was the director's "girlfriend."

On another occasion in Los Angeles, I met with a well-known producer at a famed restaurant in Beverly Hills. He was so "important" that his assistant kept interrupting our lunch to tell him some big news about a film. I thought I would "wow" him at our meeting by showing him I wasn't just any actress like the rest. I had brains and film ideas. Before long, I realized he wasn't impressed or even taking me seriously as he had only one thing on his mind, and I was NOT interested. I chose to never see him again, and I knew in the depths of my heart that I had so much more to offer.

As I continued on with audition after audition, it became nearly impossible to differentiate myself. I would look to my left and find someone who could be my twin sister standing next to me. Then I would look to my right, and that person also looked like she could be my twin. There was so much competition and comparison, and we all tried to look and act like each other.

I noticed we would study what the other actresses were wearing, and at the next audition, I would see some familiar faces. We'd often be in almost the same outfit with our hair styled the same way and with the same color lipstick on. It made it difficult to stand out. And I didn't realize then that the very thing that sets us all apart is being fully alive in who God created us to be and living in that freedom. We all have different personalities, gifts, talents, and looks. As Saint John Paul II said, we are "unique and unrepeatable."

Nevertheless, I continued to audition and was looking forward to the upcoming pilot season for TV shows. Pilot season, every January–April, is when new shows get developed and have a chance to make it to the mainstream. I had auditioned the previous year and was disappointed I didn't get a role but wanted to try again. So I was over the moon to get an audition for a nighttime soap opera, and shortly after, they wanted me for a callback. Then, I received the phone call of a lifetime saying I had booked one of the lead roles, and it felt like winning the lottery. I was jumping up and down with joy and gratitude as it was a dream come true—or so I thought.

At my first rehearsal, I met the rest of the cast, the director, and some of the producers as we read through the script. I also met my co-star, who was to play my love interest on the show. He was very handsome, with an athletic build, blond hair, bluish-green eyes, and a mesmerizing smile. It was a long day, and during our breaks, we grabbed coffee and snacks from the craft service table. We talked about our acting journeys, agents, and other interests. He seemed exceedingly nice and charming.

At the end of the day, he asked if I wanted to share a cab ride home because my apartment was on the way to his. Since I was enjoying our conversations, I willingly agreed. However, shortly after we entered the taxi and the driver got on the freeway, my co-star gave him a $50 bill and said, "Keep driving until I tell you to stop." The cab driver happily took the money, while I was very confused about what was going on. So many fears immediately rushed through my mind. *Where are they taking me? Is he going to kill me? Will I ever see my family again?*

I quickly tried to evaluate the situation and wanted to jump out but knew I couldn't. The doors were locked, and I probably would have died if I had tried to open the door. We were going fifty-five miles an hour in a middle lane with traffic all around us. If only the people in the cars going by knew what was happening. If only they could call someone to help me, but no one even noticed. As is typical in New York City, everyone was in a rush to get somewhere. Then, during the trip, he sexually assaulted me; I felt so afraid of him and was terrified. It's like he turned into a completely different person.

To my relief, the cab driver finally brought me home, and I was grateful that I had survived. But I stumbled out of the cab dazed, dumbfounded, and in complete disbelief. Before they pulled away, the actor said to me, "You know you want me, and what did you expect given how you are dressed?"

At the time, I had no idea how provocative my outfit was and certainly had not wanted this to happen. I wish I had better understood the value of modesty and how visual men are. But my immodest clothing did not make the assault my fault, and what happened was certainly UNACCEPTABLE. My mind was spinning, as I couldn't understand how someone who looked so handsome and seemed intelligent could do something like this and then try to blame me.

The next day, as anger settled in, I informed the producers about the incident and told them that I couldn't do the show if he would be my co-star. There was no way I could see him again. They would have to re-cast his role, or I would need to leave. The producers said, "He would NEVER do something like that." They made me feel like I was lying—as if I had made it up!

Absolutely crushed, I had a very difficult decision to make. Ultimately, I decided to leave the show because I couldn't imagine having to play my assaulter's love interest and kiss him on camera. My dream had been shattered. I felt so ashamed and alone that I never even told another soul or processed the event until over fifteen years later. I guess I thought it was easier to forget what had happened than to deal with the pain. To be numb seemed better than feeling enraged about my broken dream and how powerless I felt in the situation.

On the outside, I hid behind yet another mask layer and appeared more assured than ever—full of pride, independent, and self-sufficient. I didn't need anyone because I didn't trust anyone and vowed I would never be vulnerable again.

People who knew me said I was tough, fearless, and powerful—someone who went after whatever she wanted and got it. However, that couldn't have been further from the truth, as it was fear that held me in bondage to this façade.

After my return to the Catholic Church, I remembered the event in the taxi and finally had the courage to tell a priest about it. I shared it not because I had sinned, but because I felt safe with him. When I brought this darkness to the light, the result was freedom from chains of bondage, and I experienced such incredible relief as if unbearable weights had been lifted off me.

It felt good to have someone acknowledge that what had happened to me was wrong. And as I began to go deeper in the forgiveness of this man, I wondered if he had done the same thing to other women. If so, how many were before or after me?

I have since studied *Theology of the Body*,[3] a series of 129 talks by Saint John Paul II. It discusses how the mystery of God is revealed through the human body and the beauty of our sexuality. I also completed my certification in the "Catechesis on Human Love" and taught the certification classes at the local diocese for several years. Nationally, I speak frequently on this topic, and it has become a great source of redemption.

What I've learned is that our sexuality is sacred, and the body is beautiful. However, the enemy seeks to twist and destroy something so good to turn it for evil. God gave us our sexuality as light, but lust, selfishness, and pornography turn it into darkness. This darkness spreads to try to hide the light—the original beauty God gives to all of us.

I realize now that pornography is likely to blame for this young man's bondage and selfishness. True love wills the good of the other. However, pornography uses another person for one's own selfish gratification, despite the cost to the other person and their heart.

Saint John Paul II said, "The problem of pornography is that it does not reveal too much of a woman but too little," because it does not show a person for who they truly are but instead objectifies them.

The enemy isn't stupid either. He knows we are judged on love and that love is a relationship. He is terrified of our bodies and our beauty and what the world would look like if we all loved one another. The intense longing in our hearts that gets distorted is an intense longing for God. It's a desire for deep intimacy and union—to be known, to be loved, and to give and receive one another. The enemy twists goodness for just a moment of pleasure instead of leading us to the ultimate fulfillment, which is spiritual ecstasy in heaven. In heaven, we won't need sex because we will be in union with God and one another—a perfect marriage of hearts. Marriage and spousal union here on earth are just tiny glimpses and foretastes of heaven. And because we are body and soul, we need to remember that sexual union here is not just two bodies coming together but also two hearts.

Additionally, men are created to be very visual and take in a woman's beauty. They are driven by a need for affirmation, honor, and respect. Yet pornography does the opposite. It distorts the good and hurts the hearts of others. And it's not only men that are addicted, as studies show the number of women being lured to pornography is also rising.

Usually, many other factors and wounds lie underneath all of this, along with a fear of intimacy. We are created for intimacy with God and one another, but often things happen that cause fear to get in the way. I wanted to affirm, honor, and respect my co-star, but he never gave me a chance. He took from me instead and hurt my heart as well as his own. Men are created to be protectors and heroes, though many have just forgotten.

I think I may have also found a potential cure for pornography. Men, by nature, want to be good lovers. Pornography damages relationships and makes them terrible lovers as most of it is violent and disrespectful. Men will never be respected or honored for treating women like this in real life. In these fantasy scenes, the women are paid to pretend they enjoy it. But if a man wants to be a good lover, he will turn to Christ and see what real sacrificial love is. He will strive for a deep and intimate relationship with his spouse and be a good leader—someone she wants to follow. Only then will he really feel satisfied and be the hero he longs to be, one free from shame and guilt.

Sometimes, God also allows severe temptations in the spiritual life, but He provides a way out with each one. When resisted and with every battle won, the heart becomes more purified and loves more deeply. To suffer with God instead of leaving Him out can save many souls. I share this because I know people suffering from these temptations and not always winning. But the times that they do are a huge victory for the Kingdom, and I can't think of many things more fulfilling in our lives than our sexuality. What greater offer can there be but to love purely for the sake of God. He created sex and made it to feel good, but it's designed to be free, total, faithful, and fruitful within the commitment of marriage.

By grace alone, I have forgiven my co-star, and I still pray for him. The experience fuels my fire to share what real love is and to insist that we should never settle for a counterfeit. I thank God for redeeming my heart and placing a fire inside me to help others.

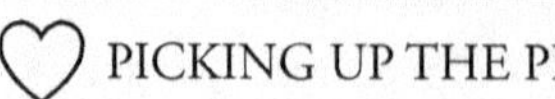 PICKING UP THE PIECES

How have you handled broken dreams in the past? Has something terrible ever happened to you that you have forgotten about for some time or have hidden from others? Where might shame be hiding in your heart? Have you put on a mask to cover the pain? Are you ready to face it and be set free? Are you prepared to let God restore your heart and dreams?

PRAYER

Lord Jesus, please heal the deep wounds in our hearts that others have inflicted on us by seeing us as an object of use and not as a person. Please forgive us for using others in our past as well. Please heal us and help us help others by turning our pain into our passion for setting captives free. Amen.

CHAPTER 13

FAITHFUL WITNESSES

Love is patient, love is kind. It is not jealous, [love] is not pompous,
it is not inflated, it is not rude, it does not seek its own interests,
it is not quick-tempered, it does not brood over injury, it does not
rejoice over wrongdoing but rejoices with the truth.
It bears all things, believes all things, hopes all things,
endures all things. Love never fails.
—1 Corinthians 13:4–8

After so many wounds of un-love, I began to reflect on times when I'd encountered pure love. We all long to belong and be in the Father's house, and our homes and hearts should be reflections of His love. However, after the fire and all that had happened, my relationship with my parents grew increasingly strained and emotionally vacant. Our home was filled with intense suffering, anger, and bitterness.

Thankfully, my wonderful aunts and uncles invited me to their homes often. And all week long, I looked forward to our "Pasta Sunday" at my grandparents' house. The whole family, except my father, would meet there and share an unbelievable meal and spend time just being together.

My grandmother's meat sauce was incredible too—it was difficult not to go for seconds! And my grandparents loved having us all there as our time was filled with warmth and affection. Their house was a refuge and a rock in my life.

In addition to throwing me into the confessional, Grandma and Poppy treated me as their own child and showed me what love really looks like. They exemplified a deep and holy love for one another, which was beautiful to witness.

Grandma lost her father when she was fourteen months old and her mother when she was eight, so her aunt and uncle took her in. Tragically, her stepfather shot and killed her uncle, and her aunt was then left alone to raise fourteen children—they all grew up poverty-stricken. The loss of her parents and uncle was devastating, but in her depression, my grandmother chose to run to church and to the Blessed Mother for spiritual adoption. She found peace with her in moments of despair.

Grandma walked to school and church so often that she had to go to the town poormaster to get a new pair of shoes. Back then, they didn't have social services like we do today, and when she went to ask, sometimes the poormaster was reluctant. He would yell at her and say, "I just gave you a new pair!" She would have to lift her feet to show him the bottoms and say, "Sir, but there are holes in my shoes." Then he would begrudgingly give them to her and she would walk away in utter embarrassment and humiliation.

For food, she sometimes got the rotten bananas off the fruit cart since no one wanted them and would even eat part of the peel. Grandma was so thin that the doctor said he could hang a clothesline from one rib to the other as her stomach was sunken in. However, she persevered in prayer, and one of the things she prayed for daily was for a prince to rescue her. Grandma desired a holy husband, and that prayer was eventually answered.

The day she met Poppy, it was love at first sight, and she said, "That's the man I'm going to marry!" Poppy, an Italian immigrant, came from a hardworking family that did very well financially. They were also deeply rooted in the Catholic faith. He fell in love with my grandmother, and they got engaged after Midnight Mass on Christmas in front of the statues of the Sacred Heart of Jesus and Our Blessed Mother.

He happily worked three jobs to provide for the family and read his Bible during his lunch break. Poppy was very close to the Lord, and I was eventually given the Bible that he read daily—it's one of my greatest treasures. The pages are worn and well-loved, but not only did he read it, he walked the talk. He lived the Gospel and was a true disciple of Jesus. Poppy gave to those in need, loved deeply, and was quick to forgive whenever someone wronged him.

He was a simple but very happy man. His favorite pastime was being at home with the family in the living room laughing together just after our big Italian meal. And my aunts, uncles, cousins, and I would gather around him as he told jokes. He often cracked himself up while he was trying to tell them and sometimes could barely get the joke out. We would laugh at him laughing because it was so cute, but he thought we were laughing at the jokes—which made him laugh even louder. Poppy said life was too short not to laugh and he would also joke around and say, "If you're ever in trouble, just mention my name." Now that he's passed and is in heaven, I understand what he meant. Even if I thought he was just kidding at the time, those very words have become prophetic, as I believe he is a great saint and intercessor.

Grandma was a fantastic homemaker and one of the best cooks I've ever known. She served her family with great delight and always told everyone and anyone that Poppy was her prince. She had a deep respect and reverence for him, and indeed he was her hero who showered her with love and attention.

Poppy often told her, "Get whatever you want. You have the checkbook," because he trusted her so much. She never had holes in her shoes again and wrote her first book at age eighty-five, titled *No More Holes in My Shoes.*[4] She bravely shared her story of the trial that turned into triumph. It's a real-life Cinderella story with God right in the middle of it. My grandma brought hope to so many people as she clung to God during her darkest moments, and she always had her eyes on the resurrection.

Venerable Father Patrick Peyton said, "A family that prays together stays together." I'm not saying my grandparents never yelled at each other or got into a fight. That wouldn't be a reality for anyone, but I will say that they never went to bed mad. Poppy couldn't hold a grudge even if he wanted to, and any argument they had was usually over something minimal.

Toward the end of his life, Poppy always wanted Grandma by his side. Even if she left to go down the street to get the mail, he would say, "I prayed for you the entire time. Thank God you're back!" He also began to lose his appetite in his later years and was afraid to tell her.

In Grandma's opinion, health was determined by how much you ate, because of what she suffered as a child, and Poppy didn't want to disappoint her. So one day, when she went to check the mail, he hid his food in the garbage under a newspaper. He told me not to tell her, but then he ratted on himself a few minutes after she walked in. He just couldn't bring himself to lie to her. It was adorable but sad, as his health was deteriorating.

They prayed several Rosaries a day together and recited the Divine Mercy Chaplet daily at 3:00 p.m. After Poppy retired, he would often be relaxing in his recliner, and when I looked at him, I would see his lips moving. When I asked what he was doing, he would say, "I'm praying," as he was in constant prayer. He was a man who would give the shirt off his back to the poor and to anyone who asked or looked in need. He gained everything by giving it away and was unattached to the things of this world.

Poppy was a very handsome Italian man, with olive skin and bright green eyes that were filled with the love and kindness of Christ. He often wore his old polyester pants, a white T-shirt, and a cardigan and hardly ever spent money on himself.

I still have one of his cardigans that he wore almost every day, and it has a little hole on the sleeve, but I cherish it. I put it on over my shoulders when I'm having a rough day and feel his fatherly love and protection covering me.

Poppy was always so grateful for everything he had and lived a humble life with gratitude. Their home wasn't big, but he saved up and paid cash for it. He often looked around and said, "Look at all of this. I never thought I would have so much."

He was a strong father figure for me growing up and called me his monkey as I climbed up onto his lap so that he could hold me in his arms. That's where I felt the safest and most loved. Poppy always asked me if I needed anything and would give it to me without hesitation. Many times, though, I hid my needs and insecurities from him because if he had known, he would have given me whatever I asked for.

He was also bold enough to yell at me in high school when he thought my skirt was too short, and sometimes he made me change my clothes. Poppy was a protector, provider, and the strongest man I have ever met.

We danced together at every family party. Even when he was older and could barely move, I made him get up and dance with me to the song "Twist and Shout." Of course, I also sang at all our large Italian family parties. They were significant catered events with a DJ and professional videographers. Every chance I got, I was on the videos talking and giving messages of love to my family or practicing my Italian.

In one video that I treasure, I'm dancing to "You are so Beautiful" with Poppy. Although I can't hear or remember what we were talking about, he kissed me on the head twice, showing his deep affection for me. I had an ear-to-ear smile and was radiating joy. I know he thought of me as his daughter as he knew I needed adoption and felt lost.

When he was on his deathbed unconscious, my grandma sat constantly by his side, holding his hand. Once, she had to leave the room for a few minutes and asked me to hold his hand for her. I gladly accepted, but when I did, something happened that is difficult to describe. It was a foretaste of the life-changing experience I would have several years later. I never told anyone, but somehow while holding his hand, I had a deep awareness of his purity and holiness. I also saw that I was far from the Lord and felt very repentant. Grandma returned shortly after, and I left the room stunned. Poppy was such an amazing man and had a pure love for me and all those he met. Love indeed remains when we leave for our eternal home in heaven. My grandfather's love and that experience are still with me.

Grandma, who recently passed at age ninety-four, never forgot her childhood. She was always very charitable and hated to throw food out since she had grown up so poor. Before putting any food in the trash, she always kissed it first. I learned this from her and still do the same without even realizing what I'm doing—it has become second nature to me.

My grandma made me breakfast and took me to school every day. I'll never forget her singing "Lord, You Have Come to the Seashore" in the car and belting it without a care in the world. Her voice was nasally and often off-key, but it was the sweetest sound to me. Grandma's faith was so bold she didn't care what others thought, she just made "a joyful noise."

I know the root of my grandparents' love for me stemmed from their profound relationship with the Lord through prayer and perseverance. It's challenging to live in a world where we are created for love but often experience so little of it. Saint Mother Teresa worked with the poorest of the poor, and she said, "Being unwanted, unloved, uncared for, forgotten by everybody, I think that is a much greater hunger and much greater poverty than the person who has nothing to eat." We all feel unloved at times, but the moments where we experience true love or witness it in this life are like a small glimpse into heaven. My grandparents were always a window into heaven for me. If only I had kept my eyes on what's above and held onto the witness of God's love—a love that seemed distant yet was so present through them.

 PICKING UP THE PIECES

Do you have someone in your life that has supported you when others haven't? What are your good memories of them? What did they do or say that has left an impression on you and how you live? Who has been a good role model of the faith for you? If you aren't married yet, have you prayed for a godly spouse? If you are married, are you praying with your spouse? If you are in religious life, are you praying in the community with your whole heart?

PRAYER

Lord Jesus, help us remember the people in our lives who have been positive examples of your love and mercy. May we cling to you in our time of need and trust that you have something beautiful planned and will never leave us despite our current circumstances. Lord, you know our needs. Please guide and provide. Amen.

CHAPTER 14

INADEQUACY AND INSECURITY

In the same way the tongue is a small member and
yet has great pretensions. Consider how small
a fire can set a huge forest ablaze.
—James 3:5

I'm thankful for my grandparents and all they have done for me. Although I had struggled in my relationship with my parents, they have also done nice things for me when they could. My mom insisted that I get a degree in something other than acting, and when she came into some money, she gave everything she had for my college education—for which I was very grateful.

I initially started out as an international business major because I thought it would be fun to travel the world. I also had a desire to experience different cultures and had a knack for business, but I wasn't doing well in the difficult math classes, and it just didn't feel right. I knew I should change majors but wasn't sure what to do. Then a few people suggested speech communication with a concentration in mass media, and I thought that sounded easy, so I quickly made the change. I remember taking the classes, thinking, *How will I ever use this degree for anything?* It didn't make much sense to me until years later, because back then, I couldn't see what God had in store. I didn't realize that my college classes were preparing me for my future, and God was speaking to me through others without me even knowing it.

I took classes in intercultural and interpersonal communication, along with radio and TV announcing, and got to give speeches. Often, I was surprised at how easily words flowed out of my mouth, but I didn't think much of it. I thought it was like that for most people, and I certainly had no idea that I would end up becoming an inspirational speaker one day.

During this time, I also continued auditioning for various projects. One of my agents handled TV hosting and worked at one of the most well-known agencies in New York City. He called me into the office one day with short notice to film an audition that he would send out to Los Angeles. Feeling completely exhausted, I really wasn't up for it when I went in because I had stayed up way too late the night before.

When I was done with the audition, the agent looked disappointingly at me and said, "I don't know, Joelle, you just don't have that spark; something's missing." I remember walking out of his office with my head down, feeling so defeated and depressed—like I wasn't enough. Looking back, I think he was just picking up on my mood, but I took his criticism to heart and perceived it as if I was missing something. I wondered, *How do you get a spark? Did God not equip me with that too?*

It only took one person saying something negative to plant doubt in my heart. After that, every time I went on an audition, those words stirred in the back of my mind. And they stayed with me for several years, regardless of any success I had.

Without realizing it, I allowed this person's opinion to impact me and put him on a pedestal—which is a form of idolatry. In my heart, I knew I was created for what I was doing, or I was at least headed in the right direction. However, I didn't know how to pray and ask God what He thought about it. While many others had said nice things to me over the years, this comment stuck to my heart.

We all want to be accepted and hear people affirm us in our calling, and it's great when that happens, but we also can't let one person's opinion overthrow us. God is always consistent and positive in what He tells us about our identity and mission—even correction comes with love.

Despite the hurt of these words, I'm glad I kept pursuing my passion and continued moving forward. Ironically, shortly after that incident, I booked a job as co-host for an international TV show. The show focused on the latest fashion and trends, and we covered events such as Miami Fashion Week and the glamour of New York City nightlife. It was another dream come true, but quickly, disappointment set in. I struggled with what was happening behind the scenes—the parties, drugs, and constant networking were too much for me to handle. I didn't care for these things and remember doing a late-night shoot at an after-hours club in New York. It was tough staying up all night sober and I decided it wasn't something I wanted to be a part of anymore. The people in the company were nice, but overall, the environment led me into deeper darkness.

An outfit I wore for one of the shoots was also less than fashionable, as I recall. I would say it was rather "barely there." At the time, I didn't realize how alluring it was, nor did I understand the message I was sending into the world. My desire to be seen distracted me from my immodesty.

Now, I can start to see the agent's words from another perspective. Maybe to some extent, he was right, and I took what he said the wrong way. Perhaps he could see that I was sad underneath, and something was "off." Maybe he glimpsed that I had forgotten who I was. I didn't understand it at the time, but the spark I was missing was God in my life. But what if I had let those words define me and never auditioned again? What if I had just given up? I would have never become a TV show host or speaker at all.

God has a purpose for each of us, and when we pursue Him, we will begin to see it more clearly. It may take time, but the opportunities will show up. He will redeem the hurts in our lives and use them for His glory. We can't give up on the dreams and the deep desires He places in our hearts—perseverance and trust are key.

Also, it's difficult at times to see the spark in ourselves, and we can become our own worst critics. Too often, one negative comment from someone remains while ten other positive ones go in one ear and out the other.

An invisible battle surrounds us, and we need to be aware that God has a plan for us, and the enemy's goal is to take us from that plan. There will always be a fight against our giftings. However, the beauty of this story—and trust me, my story was a long time in the making—is that when we surrender our hearts to God, everything begins to make sense.

God can use anything, and over time, our calling comes more into focus. We begin to see His hand in many places throughout our lives. He loves us and will never leave us, and we all have His spark within. It's a spark that no one can take away. That fire within us which can ignite sparks in so many people's hearts if we just let it. Let us become the fire by being true to ourselves, our callings, and the path that God has planned for us. What He says about us is all that matters.

♡ PICKING UP THE PIECES

Where might your gifting and calling be that the enemy doesn't want you to fulfill because of all the people you can help? What hurtful words have been said by others that you need to give to Jesus? What is the truth?

PRAYER

Lord Jesus, please go into our places of woundedness and heal us. Speak truth into our hearts and open our eyes to see the mission you have for us. Help us to see the gifts you've given us so that we can fulfill your plan for our lives. Amen.

CHAPTER 15

DOUBT AND FEAR

*Your adornment should not be an external one: braiding the
hair, wearing gold jewelry, or dressing in fine clothes,
but rather the hidden character of the heart, expressed in the
imperishable beauty of a gentle and calm disposition,
which is precious in the sight of God.*
—1 Peter 3:3–4

After living in New York City for nearly six years and receiving my college degree, I moved to Los Angeles to further my career. Some family members were excited for me, but not everyone was. To get me to stay in New York, one relative cornered me to share their thoughts. This person constantly criticized me growing up and often told me my hair looked messy and terrible. She also said that my ears stuck out too much and to make sure that I covered them with my hair. Because of this, I hardly ever wore my hair up and still don't show my ears often. Although I realize now that they are normal and nothing is wrong with them, it's difficult to erase these words.

When I told this person I was moving, she lashed out and said, "L.A. already has a ___________," and she named an actress well-known for having a large bottom. She was essentially telling me that there was already one of me out there, and I wasn't going to make it in the entertainment industry. I was super thin at the time, but as most models and women do, I struggled with never feeling thin enough.

Defiantly, I still moved to Los Angeles, as I've never been the kind of person that likes anyone to tell me I can't do something. I only tend to strive harder just to prove them wrong, but inside, her words cut me, creating so much self-doubt and fear. I already felt "not enough"—not "thin enough," not "beautiful enough," and not "talented enough," and she had driven a knife straight into my insecurities. So I lost weight quickly, obsessively monitored everything I ate, and got down to a very unhealthy number for five years. I ate so little that many days I had no energy to even leave the house or go to auditions. And as I quickly became more self-centered and wrapped up in the things of the world, maintaining my body image became a full-time job. It left little room to help others or for much else.

I look back at pictures from that time and remember how heavy I felt on a specific day, yet in the photo, I looked like a walking skeleton. It's interesting how distorted our thinking can be when it comes to our body image. So many people assumed that because I was a model, I knew that I was beautiful. But just because I appeared secure on the outside doesn't mean that's what I was experiencing on the inside. I felt starved not just for food but for affirmation and acceptance.

Years and years of looking at what society says is beautiful and not always being able to live up to that standard took its toll on me. I struggled for a long time until I finally surrendered my beauty and body to God.

I once heard that when companies market to women, they show skinny figures, yet they show much more voluptuous ones when they market to men. This alone tells us that what women are conditioned to think is beautiful is not the same for men. And what I have learned more and more is that what men find most attractive is a woman who is confident and comfortable in her own skin. The more we dwell on a perceived imperfection, the more we draw attention to it. However, when we are alive in who we are created to be and are comfortable with our bodies, others can see us more clearly and focus on us as a person.

When we are preoccupied with ourselves, it takes us out of the present moment. If we are worried about how our hair looks or someone noticing something we think is wrong with us, then we will not be fully present to the person right in front of us.

Dwelling on these things also causes interior pain and anxiety. However, when we release them to God, we can live in freedom. Then we can focus on what we're called to do and live with joy in our hearts. Inadequacy gets replaced with the truth that we are all unique, and all of us are enough. Since we are made in the image of God, and God is enough, then we are enough.

Saint Mother Teresa comes to mind, as so many quotes reference her beauty. Nearly anytime someone mentions her name, they talk about how beautiful she was. She is always smiling in her pictures, and her eyes are sparkling as if they are smiling too. No one ever says, "Wow, look at her wrinkles," or "Wow, look how covered up she is," or "I wonder how much she weighs." Instead, they see the true beauty and radiance that can only come from within. It is God's beauty shining through her. She was fully alive in who He created her to be, and she wasn't worried that her age was showing. Saint Mother Teresa lived a life of service fueled by an intense prayer life. The fruits of that were evident to all. She was certainly an image of true beauty and loved everyone she met.

Now, I'm not saying it's wrong to wear makeup, exfoliate your skin, exercise, or dress nicely. All of those things are part of taking care of yourself and can accentuate the natural beauty you've been given. The harm is when these things become an obsession and the object of your happiness. Are you putting on a mask to hide behind, or are you accentuating the real "you" in freedom? We are called not to conceal but to reveal, and I'm happy to say that I'm now a healthy weight and have the energy to help others.

There is freedom in surrender and accepting the truth of who we are in Christ. That is where true beauty begins because no amount of makeup can make a soul shine.

PICKING UP THE PIECES

Do you believe God makes beautiful things? Do you believe He made you? How do you define beauty? What do you think is beautiful about others you meet? Has anyone ever said something that negatively changed how you felt about your self-image? How did you respond? What lies did you believe? Are you ready to give them to God and let His truth in? Are you ready to get rid of the pieces of your false self and replace them with your true self?

To truly know how beautiful we are, we need to believe in the Father's love for us in our very depths. Open your heart to receive Our Father's love as you ponder and pray the Scripture below.

"You are beautiful in every way, my friend,

there is no flaw in you!"

—Song of Songs 4:7

PRAYER

Dear Jesus, please help reveal to us how beautiful we are in you. Show us the areas we are struggling with, and please go into those places and heal our hearts and minds. Help us to live freely and fully in the bodies we've been given, and may we give thanks and praise for them. Amen.

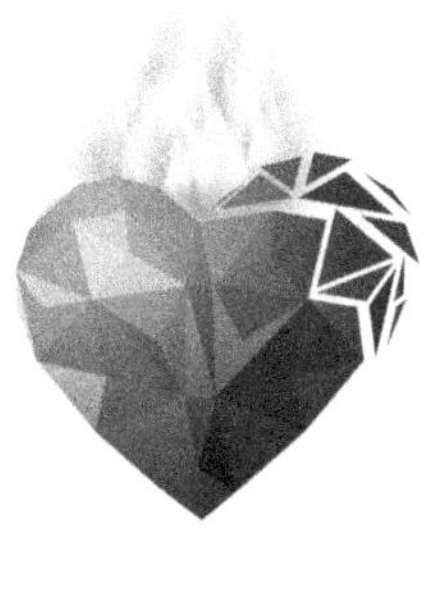

CHAPTER 16

FAILURE

This is my comfort in affliction,
your promise that gives me life.
—Psalm 119:50

My struggle with self-esteem and self-worth continued over the years. I longed for security and someone by my side to help tell me who I was. However, I didn't realize that my worth and identity are in Christ alone and that only He could fill the hole in my heart.

Because of this, during college, I left one romantic relationship for another. And a new boyfriend entered the scene after coming to my rescue over an incident with my roommate.

Even though many years had passed since the fire of my childhood, I still held an intense fear of flames. I never lit candles or had any around because they triggered the memory of the worst night of my life.

However, my college roommate was always burning candles and often left them unattended for several hours. One day, I walked into my room and saw some nearly burned down to the bottom with nothing under them. The fear of fire undid me. I became enraged and frantically went to the school authorities and begged, "Who can I speak to right now? I need a new roommate. I can't live like this!"

That night, my soon-to-be new boyfriend was the resident assistant on duty. In my vulnerability, I shared my past, and he came to my aid by helping me get a new roommate. He defended me in a bad situation, and I thought that perhaps he was the hero I had been looking for. Maybe he was the one who would finally tell me who I was, the person who would help put all of my shattered pieces back together—but that certainly is not what happened.

I had several wrong reasons for deciding to be with him. For one, I had in my head that I had to find a husband in college and could not graduate without one, because I was afraid to ever return to my abusive childhood home. The relationship also had some red flags, but I was too caught up in the fantasy of what I wanted it to be and made justifications.

We ended up getting married; however, the night before the wedding, an upsetting incident happened between us. And on my wedding day, I told one of my bridesmaids that I couldn't marry him, but she said, "Joelle, you just have cold feet. You have to go through with it."

In addition, I owed my grandparents a very large sum of money that they had lent me for the deposit on our big Italian wedding. I had no way to pay them back except from the gifts that we would receive, and many people had traveled from out of town and were staying in hotels. In all, around 250 guests were in attendance, and everyone was awaiting my arrival at the church.

It was decorated beautifully and looked like a fairy-tale wedding, yet I walked down the aisle feeling angry and confused. After the ceremony, I had to pose with my new husband for professional pictures in the church and smile like everything was okay. We did some photos acting out scenes from *Cinderella*, including one where I lost my shoe, and he found it. My dress even looked like hers, but was white, and I wore a beautiful crystal tiara on my head. On the exterior, I looked like a princess, but inside, I was furious and felt trapped. I doubted that I had actually found my true prince.

Once we finally left the church and were in the limo heading to the reception, I cried and told him how upset I was about the previous night. However, I come from a traditional Italian family that says, "Once you're married, you are together forever." This is true for the Sacrament of Marriage, but I had never heard of an annulment and didn't properly understand the sacrament. My marriage was complicated and at times very painful, and much of it I have chosen not to write about. However, I will share just a little.

Shortly after the wedding, we went on a cruise for our honeymoon, and on one of the islands, we decided to go scuba diving. I had never gone before, and they gave us a quick, fifteen-minute class before going into the water. I had no idea how serious scuba diving was, and honestly, I didn't listen well to the instructor. The only thing I did remember him saying was, "You need to always stay with your partner," and "Never leave your buddy alone."

Then we plunged into the water and went further and further down. Finally, we approached a wall of plexiglass with sharks behind it, and once we were at a significant depth, stingrays began to surround us. The instructor gave us cans of fish to feed them. And while many people thought this was fun, I was so frightened that my goggles started to fill up with tears. I could barely see and remained in fear, overwhelmed by what was going on. When I looked to the side, I realized that the entire group had left. Only some flippers could be seen off in the distance, moving swiftly away from me.

I tried to catch up, but they soon slipped out of sight. There I was, all alone, no buddy to be found. The sharks were staring at me behind the plexiglass and stingrays swarmed around me. In this moment of despair, I felt like I had no choice and did something I had been told not to do. I swam quickly to the surface and took out my mouthpiece to scream for help. But I couldn't find what I needed to press to float as I didn't remember what they had said during the class.

It was incredibly difficult to swim and keep my head above water with all of the heavy equipment and weights on—panic was setting in. I began to drown and tried reaching for my mouthpiece but couldn't find it.

Somehow I mustered all the strength I had to swim to the surface three times, yelling "HELP!" I could barely get my lips out of the water before I began to sink again. Then, a nearby instructor who was about to bring another group into the water saw me and jumped in.

I'm forever grateful that he saved my life, because as it turned out my "buddy" had gone with the group to take a picture of another couple underwater and left me behind. You can only imagine how upset I was. I could have died, and I guess you could say the honeymoon was over before it even started.

But I did my best to forget the incident and move on. I tried to look again at the bright side, thinking, *At least I have a husband*, just like I'd planned. Of course, I didn't feel like I needed advice from God or someone who might know more than me because I thought I knew it all. I felt that being married made the most sense because it sheltered me from my greatest fears—being alone, unprotected, unprovided for, and even worse, having to return to my childhood home. Yet, despite all my planning, the marriage was not what I thought it would be.

Additionally, my marriage tore me from my dreams. Acting and singing have been a part of me since I was five years old. The passion remained inside then and still does even now, but I was encouraged to leave the business, so I did. The acting industry also presented so much temptation, and many actors wanted to practice kissing scenes. As a married woman, it was difficult, because I didn't know boundaries at the time. So I agreed to give up and leave my career, which I had said I would never do. I was even on the brink of landing major jobs, including a lead role in another soap opera.

I boxed up my dreams for the time being and thought all those years were wasted, as I had no idea how God would eventually heal and resurrect them. I realize now that when we let go and let God, He brings good out of everything. Nothing and no one can ever stop His will. It's when we surrender to Him that we find our life's purpose. He purifies the desires in our hearts, so the gifts that we've been given can be used for good.

Now I realize there is extreme beauty in evangelizing through the arts—film, television, and theater. It's an amazing way to reach masses of people and introduce them to Christ. The difference is that I'm now using my gifts for God's glory. But at the time and for the sake of trying to save the marriage, I left my dreams behind—that is, until God redeemed them and spoke truth back into my heart. God puts passions in our hearts and gives us gifts for a reason. We can never get our identity from others and can only be happy being who God calls us to be.

Shortly after leaving behind my dream of acting (for the time being), I opened my first company, which was in real estate. Up late one night, I stumbled upon an infomercial and learned how lucrative it could be to fix and flip houses. I studied intensely and took one of the most difficult tests in the country and got my California broker's license. Then, I started working for a real estate company, and within a few months, I was winning top sales awards.

I quickly realized how much of my commission I was giving away, and that made no sense to me, so I started my own business. In college, I had saved up a substantial amount of cash and made a stock investment that doubled my money in one year. I was always a risk-taker, so I invested it all, and thank God it worked out.

I then used it on our first home investment, fixed up the property, and sold the home two years later for a 450 percent increase in profit. We took the proceeds and bought another home, and I subcontracted out the repairs and supervised a renovation. We then sold it nine months later and nearly doubled the investment again. As we continued to buy and flip homes in other states, the numbers increased.

Though our income was growing substantially, I was still always very concerned about money because my father had difficulty providing for the family after my sister died. Before her death, we were comfortable, but in his grief, he made some poor financial choices. He had owned a mechanic shop, but the customers weren't happy with his demeanor as he was still very angry from the fire and the loss of my sister. He also owned a lot of property where he decided to build houses but wound up selling them for less than he had planned. Sometimes our lights went off, or the phone stopped working if he didn't pay a bill.

I'll never forget the year when my school band was doing a march through the town. I played the flute (it was my sister Maria's), and my father didn't have the money to pay for the apparatus that holds the music—so he made me one. It was so much bigger and bulkier than what the others had bought, and I was devastated as other band members pointed at me and mocked me. I pretended I had asked him to make it and that I loved it, but I was very embarrassed.

No one in my town ever knew the extent of our poverty. I lived in what appeared to be a lovely home and was always dressed well, thanks to my grandparents. They gave us our home and took me shopping for school clothes every year. But because of the financial insecurity I experienced growing up, I had vowed never to be impoverished again. When I had children, I wanted to make sure that they would never suffer financially, and because of these childhood wounds, whatever the business venture was, I went into it full force. I was successful in the eyes of the world, but I didn't take time for deep and meaningful relationships the way I should have—most importantly, a relationship with God.

However, a couple of years into my new business, the real-estate market began to crash. We sold our investments and were lucky to cash out just in time. We decided to move out of California and were trying to choose where we would end up next. We thought about Tampa, Florida, and bought a house there. The home was in a double-gated community and built in the shape of the letter "U" with a pool and hot tub in the middle. The home's walls in the family room, kitchen, living room, dining room, and master bedroom completely opened up to the gigantic pool area. It was a true dream home and overlooked a magnificent golf course, but we decided not to move there because another city caught our attention.

As we were searching for where to move, we found a website where you could enter the criteria of what you were looking for in a city. Austin, Texas, kept coming up on the list, along with four other cities. We toured all of them and fell in love with Austin.

I never pictured myself going from New York to Hollywood to living in Austin, but it's a vibrant city with so much to offer. And I was excited to start over in a fresh place, though my marriage was still rocky. To numb the pain, I threw myself further into my work and even dabbled in pageants for publicity. As Mrs. Austin America, I placed fourth runner-up at the Mrs. Texas America Pageant. It was just another mask I hid behind to deflect my brokenness.

We changed homes many times during the marriage, too, and I thought that each one would fix the unhappiness in my heart. I reasoned if we just got a larger, more luxurious home, then all would be well, but of course that never worked.

We also had two beach condos in Florida and a house with a private pool near Disney World. One of our condos in Florida was right on the ocean, and when lying in bed looking out the windows, it seemed like you were floating on the sea. The lanai (porch) ran across the entire backside of the condo with walls of windows to show a breathtaking, panoramic view.

In addition, we had a condo in downtown Austin, a plot of land near the lake, and a dream home in the hill country. Our main house had a beautiful gated Italian courtyard with a castle-like appearance near the entrance and overlooked the scenic hills with a glimpse of the lake. It was built sideways with large windows so that nearly every room had a view. However, none of these properties could give me the happiness I was searching for. And the emptiness of it all only grew within me.

Of course, it's not the house that makes a home; it's the love that exists within its walls that counts. Sometimes focusing on views of the created can actually obscure our view of the Creator if we put them above Him.

The Lord eventually graced my heart with a complete detachment from the love of money and materialism as I realized it could never fulfill the deepest desires in my heart. I will share more on that later.

The bottom line is that money can't buy happiness and often does the opposite. It can also complicate life and relationships. You may start to wonder who really loves you for you or if they want to use you. It can create false suspicions of people and a fear of intimacy. Although money can certainly be used for good, when we are chasing material things in our lives thinking they will fix our broken pieces, we will eventually conclude that God alone can heal and satisfy.

Sadly, despite our beautiful homes and exterior accomplishments, my marriage was unsalvageable. It did not feel sacramental, and I filed for an annulment through the Catholic Church. God continues to redeem my life, and one of the ministries I have been delighted to serve in is a healing retreat for those going through the annulment process. I also taught marriage preparation for several years, which was a great blessing. Through teaching the courses, I learned that God can use our past to bring healing to others when we let Him.

Unfortunately, in our world today, such a high percentage of marriages end in divorce, and some people, even within the church, are less than loving to those who have suffered through it. The end of a marriage truly is a death—the death of a dream—and the grieving process takes time.

When things don't work out, it's easy to feel like a failure. We should not point fingers at others or treat the divorced like lepers. Rather, let us be a light and source of God's love to them, helping them pick up the pieces and see where things went off track.

The children of divorce also need to experience love and be embraced by the community. They need to know nothing is wrong with them and that they belong. It was not their fault! They were conceived in what was thought to be a sacramental marriage and are legitimized by the desire to love.

The moment we start judging others, we need to look within our own hearts, as no one gets married expecting it to fall apart.

What the world needs is love, not condemnation; not blame, but sacrificial love and mercy.

In the musical *Les Misérables,*[5] the character Fantine talks about broken dreams. Her life didn't turn out how she had planned, and at rock bottom, she desperately needed God's saving grace. Like Fantine, we usually begin life with an optimistic outlook and hope in God. However, as the years go by, we make wrong decisions and get caught up in sin and distractions until we can't see anymore. The enemy wants us to get stuck in shame so we can't fulfill the plans that God has for us because he knows God's plans will make us happy and lead others to Christ.

God is our dream maker and mountain shaker, and all things are redeemable in Him. When we give ourselves to the Lord, we will receive goodness back a hundredfold. No one is too far lost or too far gone for the mercy and love of God. He will continue to heal and resurrect our broken hearts.

> ♡ PICKING UP THE PIECES
>
> Do you discern relationships before getting into them and ask God what He desires for you? How can you use the wounds of your past to bring healing to others?

PRAYER

Lord Jesus, please help me to know what relationships are good for me, and please be in the middle of all of them. Please help heal my heart from anyone who has hurt me. Jesus, please take the wheel of my life and steer me in the right direction. Amen.

CHAPTER 17

PAIN AND SUFFERING

Jesus looked at them and said, "For human beings this is impossible,
but for God all things are possible."
—Matthew 19:26

After moving to Austin, my desire for children became overwhelming. Although there was great unhappiness in my marriage, I still wanted to start a family. I thought maybe if we had kids, our relationship would improve, but it didn't.

That said, my children are the best thing that has ever happened to me. And I have no doubt they are here for a reason as they are a great gift to this world. However, at the time, my marriage was at its worst.

We tried for almost two years but couldn't conceive, which left me feeling depressed and hopeless. When I went shopping and saw moms with several kids, I would be so jealous. I thought, *Lord, you gave these women so many and I'm only asking you for one. Do you not love me?*

It was painful to think that I may never have children of my own, and I know that is a reality for many couples. There are no words to explain this type of suffering as I have only tasted a piece of it myself and know how excruciating it was.

The doctors had told me I had less than a 5 percent chance of conceiving. While in one breath I was mad at God for my failing marriage, in the next, I was begging Him for a child.

Then, after years of trying, we went to see yet another specialist, and the morning we were going to meet the doctor, I had a sense that I was already pregnant. I took a test, and sure enough, miraculously, against the odds, I was! It was one of the greatest moments of joy in my life. The beauty of life and of a baby are indescribable, and my children are my greatest claim to fame beyond anything I'll ever achieve on this earth.

I could write volumes about them as I love them so much. My daughter, Siena, is very sweet, and when I asked her what her favorite color was when she was little, she said, "All of them, Mamma!" I call her my rainbow. Her first-grade teacher named her "Polite Pete" because she's so kind, and many parents have told me they want their kids to hang out with her because of her inner beauty. And while she's stunning on the outside, she knows very well that a real princess shines from within, and she does. She's also very patient and has a phenomenal voice.

My son, Blake, is hilarious and likes to make people laugh. I call him my "son" shine. He's a peacemaker who is super compassionate, talks to everyone, and never leaves anyone out. Blake is athletic and a fantastic soccer player. He also plays the trombone wonderfully.

However, despite how amazing my children are, in addition to the difficulties trying to conceive them, their deliveries were even more traumatic. With Siena, I was in the hospital in labor for over sixteen hours. The umbilical cord was wrapped around her neck, and the machine that monitored the baby's vital signs showed that her heart rate was flatlining. The jarring noise from the monitor alarm shocked me as the doctors and nurses raced into my room. They needed to move me around to help untangle the cord.

I couldn't turn on my own because I'd already had an epidural, and it was such a horrible feeling to lie there unable to do anything. They tried their best to toss my body about as the alarm continued to echo throughout the room. Finally, the doctor was able to move the cord, and her heartbeat once again showed on the monitor.

I can't explain the fear that entered in this moment. To make it that far, with this miraculous baby inside of me, and then to almost lose her just before her birth, was one of the most terrifying things I've ever lived through.

Once her heart rate steadied, they rushed me to surgery for an emergency C-section, and the doctors were able to deliver her safely. Siena looked healthy, but they told me any brain damage that may have occurred would take several years to identify. It would be hard to know until she was in preschool whether or not there was any harm from her moments without oxygen. I thank God that today she is a healthy, beautiful, and straight-A student—all is well.

We experienced a miracle yet again when Blake was also naturally conceived. However, after his delivery, I had a hernia that needed to be repaired. It had developed during my pregnancy with Siena, as my abdominal muscles had been cut during the emergency C-section. The OB-GYN told me he could repair it after this delivery. So following Blake's birth, they immediately began the surgery. The problem was that I could feel absolutely everything they were doing as I was only numbed from the belly button below and not above.

There I was on the operating table, my insides opened up, screaming in pain. The anesthesiologist had left for the day, and the only drug they could give me was one that knocked me out. It kept me from being able to vocalize what I was experiencing, but it didn't desensitize the torture or my mind. I could still feel everything and could even hear the doctor instructing an intern on how to do the procedure. He took his time, speaking very slowly, and though I was in agony, I could no longer tell them to stop.

At that moment, I had an encounter that is hard to describe, but my sister Maria and Poppy, who had passed, were there. It was like I was in a tall white room, and they were up at the top looking down at me. I didn't see their bodies but knew it was them and could feel their presence. My first thought was, *Oh my goodness, did I die on the operating table? Did they come to get me?* However, I also had an awareness that they were there to comfort me. I didn't understand everything going on at that moment as the pain was so severe. But I knew that no matter what, everything would be okay. I realized then that our loved ones never leave us; they are with us, encouraging us and giving peace amid the pain.

When I woke up and could speak again, I cried loudly, "Please give me drugs. Give me drugs. Help!" I still feel bad that was the first thing my baby saw when they brought him to me. But after the morphine kicked in, and once I held my beautiful baby boy, Blake, all that anguish subsided. He was just perfect and brought great warmth to my heart.

We all suffer moments of pain, but let's keep our eyes on life—on the precious gift of life. May we realize that every day is a gift, and that we were born for a reason. And despite all odds, we are here, born into the exact home and family that God has intended. Maybe that family isn't perfect, and terrible things may have happened, but God can turn all things into blessings in his wisdom and graciousness. I may have had a crumbling marriage; however, look what God brought out of it—two exceptionally beautiful children whom He has enormous plans for. May He be praised.

♡ PICKING UP THE PIECES

Can you look back at a time when you experienced extreme pain, whether emotionally, mentally, spiritually, or physically, and out of nowhere, peace came over you? Maybe a friend called just in time, or perhaps you were aware of the presence of a loved one that has passed away? Was there a time when you were in so much pain, whether it be emotional, mental, spiritual, or physical, and you felt like you had no one to help you or hear you but God? Let Him go into those places and fill you with hope.

PRAYER

Heavenly Father, you are the source of all life. You gave each of us life for a reason, and we are here for a purpose. Thank you for the miracle of our lives. May we live them in you, with you, and for you! Amen.

CHAPTER 18

DECEPTION

A good tree cannot bear bad fruit,
nor can a rotten tree bear good fruit.
—Matthew 7:18

Shortly after the difficult yet miraculous birth of my daughter, Siena, I started a cosmetic company. I won't get into all the details on why the company started. But I will share how I became fascinated—or should I say, obsessed—with makeup.

Beginning in elementary school, I felt very self-conscious about the freckles on my face, and by the time I got into sixth grade, I started to wear makeup. I discovered foundation and it boosted my confidence as it hid one of my greated insecurities—though the pigmentation on my face is actually very light. I'm willing to bet that anyone who has known me my entire life has probably never even noticed it. However, it's amazing how amplified our perceived flaws can become in our own minds.

In my bedroom, I had a white desk that turned into a vanity table with a mirror that flipped up on one side. I remember spending several hours examining my face and looking for imperfections. I tried many different foundation brands and colors until I found one that matched my skin tone perfectly. It didn't take long until I started to use eye shadow, mascara, blush, and lipstick as well.

Then, during my years as a model in New York and Los Angeles, I worked with some of the top makeup artists in the country and learned new application techniques. And I spent countless hours in beauty stores searching for the best products.

With an arsenal of makeup and brushes, and after reading several artistry books, I began practicing the tips on myself, friends, and family members. After I moved to Texas, people began to notice how I did my makeup and started asking me to do theirs, and they encouraged me to create a cosmetic company.

I wrestled with the idea feeling that I was supposed to do something else, but as an artist at heart, I thought a makeup company could be fun. I wish I'd known then that a lack of peace was a clear sign that I wasn't doing God's will, however, eventually, I gave in and began the new venture.

I realized I had many different brands in my makeup case, and I couldn't understand why one didn't have the best of everything. This bothered me, so I decided to create a brand where each product would become the best of the best.

This new enterprise also came with many false promises of glamour—as if the prestige of owning a cosmetic company would give me true self-worth, or I could solve the world's problems through it.

While I don't think cosmetics are "bad" and still wear makeup and enjoy it, I don't treat it as a god like I used to. The issue back then was that I no longer owned makeup, but rather, makeup owned me. It was almost like an addiction.

Then, when trying to come up with a name for the company, I came across two names in Italian that sounded good with "cosmetics." One of them meant "love" and the other meant "naughty." I felt drawn to the name that meant love, but others I asked liked the other one better, so I went with it.

However, it never felt right to me. And, after my recommitment to God, when my eyes were opened, I was saddened to see how desensitized I'd become to the message I was sending into the world.

Every time I thought about it, I felt like I had a knot in my stomach. How could I begin ministry and own a company that meant "naughty"? It bothered me so much that a couple of years after my reversion, I tried to see if I could change it, but by that time, the other name had already been trademarked. It would have also cost an exorbitant amount of money to switch it because the products were already in stamped packaging.

As part of our marketing to get around this, we would say we were "making naughty nice," but I believe it's impossible to do this. In my opinion, either it's naughty or it's nice; either it's good or it's bad—an in-between doesn't exist.

Many cosmetic companies in our culture use sensual makeup names, and the messaging becomes, "Wear this, and you'll be wanted and loved." And while makeup isn't inherently bad, it's problematic when the focus is placed on becoming an object of desire rather than being seen as a person desired for who they truly are.

In addition to being the CEO, I also became the face of the company, which put me back into modeling and the public eye. Although I did mainly beauty headshots, during some of the photo shoots, I also wore lingerie. While the shots were done tastefully, I definitely wasn't projecting the girl-next-door look, and certainly, I have my regrets and have repented.

Despite my misgivings, the company seemed successful in the eyes of the world, and many doors continued to open. The products were top-notch and some of the best on the market. Celebrities wore our makeup, and it was featured on major television networks and in mainstream magazines. They were also sold at one of the most luxurious department stores and in high-end boutiques across the country—including one on Sunset Boulevard in West Hollywood. Major online retailers carried our products too. And I was often interviewed on various news shows and at conferences. Nonetheless, I remained restless and hungry for my true purpose as I yearned for a deeper meaning in life.

Behind the scenes were also a lot of expenses and stress, and I worked some nights until 2:00 a.m. I had a cook, a nanny, full-time day care, and even someone to buy my groceries so I could focus on the company. One of my biggest regrets is all of the time that I missed with my kids. And deep down, I knew something was missing in my life. Although I continued to smile for the cameras, I didn't have true joy in my heart.

It will never feel right when we're not doing what we are created for or are misusing God's gifts and leading people in the wrong direction. We live in a culture that tries to sell the idea that naughty is nice and bad is good. But I don't believe that's possible because we are made in the image of God, who is love, and truth and love are inseparable. Anything that is not true will never fulfill us.

"Do not accept anything as the truth if it lacks love. And do not accept anything as love, which lacks truth. One without the other is a destructive lie."
—*St. Teresa Benedicta of the Cross*

Bad being good is a false promise that many fall for, and while God wanted to use my face for something, this company wasn't the right avenue.

At this point, I was caught up hiding my pain with so many masks that the layers were thick and indistinguishable. It was a lifetime of hurts, wounds, and desires that were misdirected, and now I was leading others in vain pursuits. I was once again misusing my body and beauty to sell the goods of this world. And while the lingerie I wore in the ads was beautiful, it shouldn't have been for anyone to see.

I thought that my beauty was in revealing my sexuality and didn't realize that the mystery within me was priceless. I didn't know that modesty protects our hearts and allows people to see us for who we are. I thought I would be seen and known by revealing more. But the opposite was true, and I was just being seen as an object to sell another thing.

In ministry, I've counseled women who admit they dress a certain way to get attention from men. When I explain that the attention they receive is different from what they really desire in their hearts, they understand and want to make a change. We all want the same thing; we just need the truth to go about it correctly. Truth is life, while lies and misleading others leads to death—naughty can never be nice!

 PICKING UP THE PIECES

Have you ever struggled with dark spots or imperfections on your face and become obsessed with them? How much time and energy are you spending trying to fix these things or worrying about them? Where might God be speaking to you in your life's decisions to direct you on the right path? Where is your true peace?

PRAYER

Dear Jesus, please help us to know your will and give us the grace and strength to do it. Help us to not be insecure about our perceived imperfections but rather surrender them to you. Please help us to know our true worth and beauty and that we are not alone. Please redeem any of our past mistakes and lead us in the right direction. Amen.

CHAPTER 19

IDENTITY LOSS AND TRAUMA

The LORD rebuilds Jerusalem, and gathers the
dispersed of Israel, Healing the brokenhearted,
and binding up their wounds.
—Psalm 147:2–3

What I wanted was true joy and to know my purpose. But when you're living a lie and know something is missing, a nagging feeling inside coupled with a lack of peace tells you, *No, this isn't it; you were created for more.* And without a life of prayer, it's nearly impossible to know what to do.

By this point, I was in a state of utter brokenness. It culminated from a lifetime of experiences that shattered my heart into a million little pieces. On top of that, painful memories from my past that I had tried to bury began coming up and affecting me—

both physically and emotionally. A couple of events in particular are very difficult to write about, but they are an important part of my story, so I will share them.

During my time in Hollywood, I had an intense argument with someone whom I thought I knew well. However, it turned out they weren't who I thought they were. During the disagreement, this person ferociously wrapped their hands around my neck and began strangling me, almost to the point of me losing consciousness. I can still see their big brown eyes filled with hatred and rage, nearly bulging out of their head as they tried to take my life. The room began to spin around me as I struggled to breathe, and the more I fought back, the tighter the grip became.

I was initially shocked by the violence of someone I had trusted. However, I was so lost at the time, that I remember making a choice to not even fight back anymore. Maybe it was instinctive, but I also secretly thought I deserved to die as I wasn't sure why I was living anyway.

Lying there perfectly still, I felt my heart racing within me, like it would beat right out of my chest. I was playing dead, but truly, was already dead inside. After years of diving into the roles and lives of different characters in the acting world, I had completely lost my identity as a beloved daughter of God.

Suddenly, the person finally stopped, although I'm not sure why. Maybe they came to their senses because I didn't fight back, or I wasn't giving them the result they hoped to achieve. I wondered, *Do they just want to make me afraid of them, exert control over me, or take my life?* I'll never know the real reason, but as they walked away, I remained stunned.

The interior pain of someone wanting to kill you is indescribable. My neck was raw and red, and my skin developed black and blue fingerprints that took a long time to go away. Each day was a reminder of what had happened, and I could barely look in the mirror. And as an actress in Hollywood, whose job description was to appear flawless, I was so embarrassed and ashamed.

I couldn't mentally process this encounter and only told a few people about it right after. But then, I decided to choose forgiveness and didn't speak about it again for a very long time. I realize now that I should have reported it and that it was not okay. And I wish I had the understanding and strength at the time to deal with this justly—but I was so lost.

Then, several years later, another life-changing violent incident occurred. An acquaintance, who happened to be a big, burly man, began saying terrible things to me that didn't even make sense. While many would have been afraid of him, I stood up for myself, and in my anger, I shoved him and said, "Don't talk to me like that."

In a complete rage, he came at me with all his heavy weight and power and threw me into a rock-hard surface, which was only about three feet away. My lower spine landed with such an immense impact that I immediately collapsed on the floor. I couldn't feel my legs and was paralyzed—not just emotionally and mentally, but physically paralyzed.

I remember thinking, *Will I ever walk again? Could my ability to walk be taken away from me for life?* One fight, one moment—how quickly things can change.

Fear began to set in as I wasn't sure what the outcome would be, and I don't remember much after that because it was so traumatic. But I believe within about five minutes I was able to move my legs and spent a few days in bed recovering.

As I lay in bed, my arm stopped working and I couldn't move it. Beginning to have a panic attack, I wondered if I would lose the use of my limbs permanently. So I finally decided to go to the emergency room. I forgot most of what they told me, although they assured me I wasn't going to be paralyzed as all of my reflexes were working and responding normally. Then, without realizing it, I buried the memory and moved on with my life. I thought, *What's done is done, and at least I can walk again.* That's all that mattered to me at that moment.

Consequently, years later, I began to struggle more with back pain, not knowing why. When bending over to do something simple like tie my shoe, my back would go out. I would tell myself, *Oh, wow. You must be getting old*—yet I was still young.

The pain was chronic, but I had learned to live with it. I just assumed it was normal and thought everyone suffered as they got older. It was easier for me to make excuses and tell myself lies rather than remember what had happened—that is, until the pain became unbearable.

I tried to lift something that wasn't even that heavy and could barely walk for days. Finally, I saw a doctor, and he took X-rays. I'll never forget him saying, "Here at the bottom of the spine, there's a little break. That is the foundation of the house, and the walls of the house can't stand straight if the foundation isn't strong."

I said, "Excuse me. Did you just say my back is broken?" And he looked at me with all seriousness and said, "Did you not know? It looks like there's been an injury to the area. Most people I see with something like this have been through a major impact.

Maybe it was a sports injury or something else?" Immediately, the memory pulled up, and I remembered the fight, and all of the emotion and hurt came up with it. My back was broken. Not just my spirit, not just my heart, but physically, I was broken.

Our lives are fragile, and our bodies are fragile. I had never had a broken bone in my life. But here I was—broken. Fractured. How could someone have done this to me? How could I forgive? How could I forget now that the outcome was so clear? How could I give this to God? How could this be redeemed?

After my reversion, when I had re-established my relationship with the Lord, I chose to give Him my pain. I make the choice every morning to believe that I'm not a victim and focus on being thankful that I can walk.

I can't live with a victim spirit because that will keep me down, and God has plans for me. He has plans for all of us, and no matter what our pain and suffering is and no matter what happens to us in this life, we can't stay down. We must get up and rise with Christ—there is no other choice.

Taking time to pray, I contemplated how my spiritual backbone was broken long before my physical one. I had grown weak and powerless to get in a position where someone could do something like this, as I had no self-worth or self-esteem left. Yet, to the world, it looked like I was at the top of my game.

It took a long time to work through the emotional, mental, spiritual, and physical impact that this event had on my life. And I have opted not to do surgery as I can still walk and feel much better.

While I used to go to the doctor twice a week, I haven't had to go in several years now. I'm beginning to believe that healing has occurred as the pain is not nearly what it used to be.

One of the hardest things to deal with is that I'm not supposed to ride horses, which was a dream of mine. But I still go sometimes and usually get stuck with a slow horse—call it Divine Providence.

I had to die to the things I couldn't do and embrace the things I could with new strength. I learned to train mentally like an athlete and focus on the present. I chose to surrender this to God, let go of the interior hurt, and give it to Him for His justice.

I can't say that I never have pity parties, but when people see me, I hope they see joy because I've united my pain with the cross of Christ. While I can't change that I'm suffering and can't turn back time, I can change how I respond to the pain.

At the time this event happened, I know I wasn't a perfect person—far from it—but why was this allowed? The truth is that God doesn't desire any suffering for us. He loves us so much that He gives us free will. We can use that freedom to make choices that build people up or tear people down, choices that give life or bring death.

While we can't erase what happens to us, we can choose to believe that God did not will this and wants to bring us relief. He wants us to unite our suffering with His because His burden is light. A consoling Scripture says that God collects every tear, and our tears here won't be wasted.

*"My wandering you have noted; are my tears not stored in your flask,
recorded in your book?"*
—*Psalm 56:9*

Our treasure will be in heaven. Let us choose today to believe. To believe in a God who loves. To believe in a God who redeems. To believe in a God who wants to speak truth into our lives. He wants us to not be down and crucified, but to be raised to new life in Him. To be raised to a new way of thinking, and to love Him in spirit and truth.

*"You shall love the Lord, your God, with all your heart, with all your
soul, and with all your mind."*
—*Matthew 22:37*

We can only accomplish this with grace as the mind is always the last to follow. As Saint Joan of Arc said, "All battles are first won or lost, in the mind." The mind is the battlefield, and we need to trust that God will bring good out of our greatest darkness. He can help us turn our pain into His passion, and we can inspire others to do so the same and become walking miracles.

To be honest, I suppressed much of my past for a long time. I believe it resulted as my mind and heart tried to protect themselves from a life of many traumas. But as I began to bring my broken pieces to the Lord, He brought all of my darkness to the light. By remembering these terrible moments, my memories have become transformed by the light of Truth as God suffers with me.

No matter what battles you've been through, God loves you. He loves all of us, cries with us, and collects our every tear. By renewing our minds and allowing Christ to heal our memories, they all become about Him and how He wants to use our past to help others. Even if we don't share our stories, we can relate to other people in their pain. We can offer a shoulder for someone to cry on or a smile that brightens their day.

We have all been broken in some way, and our Identity in Christ is our backbone. He is our foundation and the strength to the entire structure of our being.

 PICKING UP THE PIECES

Have you ever felt paralyzed emotionally, spiritually, mentally, or physically? Who has hurt you that you need to forgive? What pain and trials do you need God's grace to deal with right now?

PRAYER

Dear Jesus, in this world, people hurt us in so many ways. We give you our wills to forgive them and trust in you for justice. Please give us the strength and grace to get through these dark times. Amen.

PART 3
RESTORED

CHAPTER 20

LOVE OF OUR FATHER

So I tell you, her many sins have been forgiven;
hence, she has shown great love. But to one to whom
little is forgiven, loves little.
—Luke 7:47

With a broken back, broken spirit, and broken life, I finally hit rock bottom with nowhere to go but up. When I finally "made it" to what appeared to be my mountaintop moment at the rooftop photo shoot in Hollywood, my soul was shattered. I left there questioning everything about who I was and what I wanted my life to stand for. Just after that—after years of my heart being smashed into so many pieces—the Lord, in His mercy, gave me the experience I shared where I saw the state of my soul. This was the turning point in my life where I received another chance to love and serve Him.

After that moment, my entire life began to change. The new fire the Master of my pieces placed inside of me started to grow, and I pondered many things, such as, *Why am I here? What was I created for? What are God's plans? How can I fill my good column? How can I be who God created me to be, and how can I start to lead people in the right direction?*

I had a comfortable brown leather chair with an ottoman in my cozy home office, and it soon became my "prayer chair." In addition to my new conversations with God, I immediately started to read the Bible and couldn't put it down. I was surprised that the answers to all of the questions I had ever had in life were in there and wished I had read it sooner. Day and night, I reached for it, hungering for the truth, and read the entire Bible in two months.

The Lord was definitely working in my heart, and I began to gain strength in Him. However, the enemy also did not want to let go of me so quickly. I don't want to give the false impression that I had an encounter with God, turned my life around, and faced no pushback from the enemy. Because the truth is that he attacked me mightily, wanting to keep me down and continuing to remind me of my sins. He does that to all of us and is known as the accuser. He likes to condemn us, make us live in false identities, and cause us to think that God would never really use us. I then found myself suffering in a deep battle within my heart for over five months. Still longing for belonging, I didn't know where to go or what to do as I had so many unanswered questions.

I hadn't returned to the Catholic Church yet. But when I read in the Bible about young Jesus being lost and then found in the temple, a desire grew inside of me. I wanted to be in the temple like He had been, listening to the teachers. As I contemplated where this temple might be, the Catholic Church kept coming to mind. So I made a firm agreement with God and myself to start going to daily Mass because I needed to hear the truth and begin to live it.

Of course, it took some time before I actually came through on my promise. I made excuses every morning, and many distractions kept me from getting there, but within a couple of weeks, I finally went.

The first time I walked into the church, I nearly gasped at the beauty. I'm not sure why I didn't see it before, but it's as if the walls, stained-glass windows, and statues were emanating rays of light. I knew I wasn't in a worldly place; rather, it felt as if I was beginning to see into heaven. Experiencing a deep feeling of peace that I hadn't felt in many years, I realized I was finally home and where I was supposed to be all along. I was in my Father's house.

One of my greatest regrets, in addition to time lost with my children, is all of the Masses and Holy Communions I missed over the years. As I returned to the Eucharist, I had also forgotten many of the church's teachings. I didn't know that you're supposed to go to Confession before receiving Communion if you have mortal sin on your soul. However, God is merciful, and through receiving the Eucharist, He put it on my heart to go to Confession for the first time in over twelve years. My last one had been when my grandmother threw me in by my hair!

I decided to prepare for a general Confession and wrote down every sin I had ever committed in my life since I couldn't remember what I had confessed in the past. Then, by the grace of God, I worked up the courage to go.

As I stood in line waiting, I felt anxious and afraid, but I knew there was no turning back. I needed to give my past to God so that I could keep moving forward. When it was finally my turn, I entered the small, secluded room as if I was walking on a plank about to jump into the sea. The water I was jumping into, though, was the ocean of mercy.

I then sat opposite the priest, who looked intently at me. He could see that I was troubled, and my tears immediately started flowing. I could barely read what I had written on the paper and struggled to breathe as my sins seemed so grave to me. But somehow, I got through it and was relieved to be done with my list. I felt lighter for the moment and thankful that I never had to repeat any of it ever again.

It was a very long Confession, but the priest was so kind. He also warned me before I left that the enemy would tell me I wasn't forgiven and would continue to try to make me remember my sins. However, he said, "God had forgiven you. He forgives, and He forgets. You have been made new in Him."

When I left there, I wanted to believe him so badly, but exactly what he said would happen quickly did. I just wasn't strong enough in my faith yet and fell back into darkness that week. In my mind I knew that I had been forgiven, but I didn't believe it in my heart just yet.

So I decided to return the next week and confess my unbelief, as I knew I didn't need to repeat what I had already confessed.

However, this time, I fasted and prayed beforehand because I read in the Scriptures that fasting and prayer are extraordinarily powerful for healing.

Even though I was forgiven and peace was returning, it seemed like a dark cloud was following me. I still felt regretful of my past and just wanted to let it all go and give it to God. But I didn't know how to do that.

At home that night, I fell to my knees beside my bed and cried like never before, truly repenting of my sins. I didn't realize that repentance is not just "I'm sorry" followed by sorrow. If we get too stuck in sorrow, it weighs us down. That's not repentance at all, but rather a trap from the enemy. True humility, sorrow, and repentance say, "I don't want to do these things again. By your grace, Lord, I am turning away from these things. By your grace, Lord, I'm not going to put myself in these situations anymore. By your grace, Lord, I submit my life to you. I surrender to you. You are the Lord of my life. I need you for everything, and I'm done trying to go on my own path. I'm done trying to make my own shortcuts. I want to be on the path to heaven. Please help me." The Greeks call this metanoia. It's a change in the heart that leads to a change in how you live your life.

I think of Mary Magdalene, who cried at the feet of Jesus and bathed his feet with her tears and wiped them with her hair. She kissed His feet and anointed them with oil. I can imagine how dirty they were from walking on the dusty roads. And she probably knew what others thought of her as well, yet she didn't let it affect her. Her gratitude and desire to praise God overwhelmed her senses, and her eyes were fixed on Christ. Then, Simon began to judge her, but Jesus could see her heart and defended her. It's true that the one who is forgiven much, loves much. She wanted to give all of herself to Jesus at that moment, and nothing else mattered. Then He forgave her and redeemed her past, giving her a restored identity in Him. He said the powerful words, "Your sins are forgiven . . . Your faith has saved you; go in peace" (Luke 7:48, 50).

Repentance, faith, and forgiveness all go together and lead us toward freedom. I had finally reached a deep state of repentance and opened my heart to receive God's love and forgiveness. However, I also realized I needed to forgive myself. Sometimes forgiving ourselves and trusting in God's goodness is the hardest part. But we find our serenity in surrendering and believing in His love and mercy. So I offered it all to God, choosing to forgive myself as Christ forgave me, and continued to pray through the tears and suffering I was experiencing.

As I knelt beside the bed in my darkened room with only the nightstand lamp on, I fiercely desired to have light within. I wailed, screamed, and cried out to God from my depths while in a battle with the enemy who was still after my soul. He was trying to clutch it out of the hands of God through condemnation and fear. The darkness and interior struggle created severe spiritual pain and anguish.

As I continued to repent and pray in the most profound agony, I was shocked to hear the words, "Abba, Abba," fly out of my mouth, which pierced my heart. Having read the Bible only once at this point, I didn't remember the Scripture that says:

"For you did not receive a spirit of slavery to fall back into fear, but you received a spirit of adoption, through which we cry, 'Abba, Father!' The Spirit itself bears witness with our spirit that we are children of God, and if children, then heirs, heirs of God and joint heirs with Christ, if only we suffer with him so that we may also be glorified with him."
—Romans 8:15–17

I continued to pray passionately, "Abba, please put me into the arms of Jesus. I want all of this darkness to lift. I am yours and belong to you!" Then, at that moment, I saw the Lord Jesus appear in His glory. The image will be forever impressed on my mind and heart. A gorgeous bluish-green color that I've never seen before was luminously shining all around Him. I saw Him with His heart on fire like the image of the Sacred Heart, and He appeared as a fortress over me. He radiated majesty, and it was apparent, without a doubt, that He truly is King of Kings and Lord of Lords. I saw that He is sovereign, and there is nothing above Him or His love. For His strength is derived from Love, which He is, and no weapon, person, or entity could ever overcome it. His hands were down with great power pouring out via rays of the brightest and purest light, and a love I had never felt before immediately flooded me, along with a peace that surpasses all understanding.

I fell back against my bed and rested in Him, and those dark clouds and heaviness lifted off me and left the room. It was as if God just blew the darkness away. At that moment, I knew He had utterly delivered me from my past and had given me a second chance. He gave me a new heart, a heart that would never be the same—a heart on fire for the things of God. I could never forget how much I had been forgiven.

Saint John Paul II said, "We are not the sum of our weaknesses and failures. We are the sum of the Father's love for us and our real capacity to become the image of His Son Jesus." I didn't understand how much God our Father loves us, or how real He was until that moment. Our Daddy, "Abba," not only hears our cries but also delivers us from all evil.

So many times, it feels as if evil has a hold on us because the devil likes to appear like he's much bigger than he really is, but he is a created being. God is the Creator. Nothing stands above God and nothing and no one could ever keep us away from His love.

"For I am convinced that neither death, nor life,
nor angels, nor principalities, nor present things, nor future things, nor
powers, nor height, nor depth, nor any
other creature will be able to separate us from the love of
God in Christ Jesus our Lord."
—Romans 8:38–39

I don't like how horror films glamorize evil; I think it's all a setup to create fear in people by making the enemy look so big and strong. I tell you with everything I have, at that moment in my bedroom, I saw that absolutely nothing could stand against the power of God. The only power the enemy has is the power we give him. Nothing can touch us when we close the doors to sin and enter the Father's house and call him Abba. We are made new, and God opens new doors in our lives, and His plan begins to reveal itself.

We are called to be "Children of Light." If we can shine a light in the darkness, the darkness doesn't stand a chance. But, so often in this world, we let the darkness take advantage of us when we seek healing, love, and our identity in all the wrong places. What if it was as simple as seeking those things in God and being affirmed in Him? What if it was as simple as not looking to others and material things to fill a void that only He can fill?

How can we become Children of Light in this dark world that so desperately needs it? I believe the answer is getting on our knees, turning away from our past sins, and crying out, "Abba." Our redemption is in knowing who our Father truly is.

One of my favorite quotes is, "Don't tell your daddy how big your problems are. Tell your problems how big your daddy is." Our Father can move mountains, and if He hasn't answered our prayers yet, it's because He has something better for us. What we think is good may not be His will, or it may not be the right timing. However, God's timing is always perfect. His ways are above our ways, and He can see what we cannot. What if life was just so simple as to call out to our Abba and trust that He will answer us and work all things together for our good?

"We know that all things work for good for those who love God, who are called according to his purpose."
—*Romans 8:28*

 PICKING UP THE PIECES

What is your relationship like with God our Father? How do you envision Him? How do you envision Jesus? When was the last time you sought forgiveness for your sins? Have you truly repented from past sin, or are you just going through the motions? Do you believe that you are truly forgiven, or have you been stuck in shame and regret?

PRAYER

Abba, Father, help us to know your love and trust in you. Protect us and deliver us from all evil. Please help us to rest in the power of your love and mercy. Thank you for always desiring to give us what is best for us even when we don't realize it. Amen.

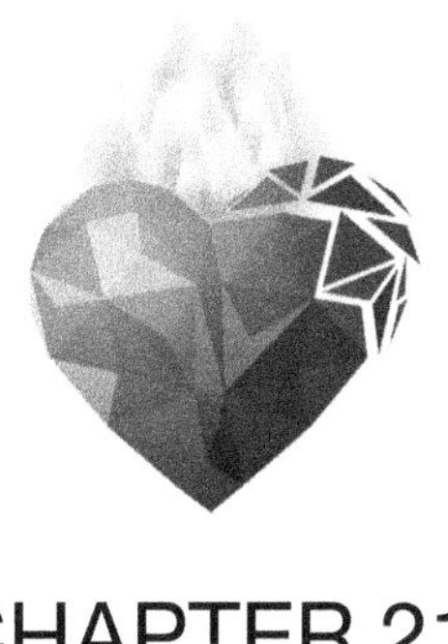

CHAPTER 21

GOD'S PRESENCE

So whoever is in Christ is a new creation: the old things have passed away; behold, new things have come.
—*2 Corinthians 5:17*

With strength returning to my soul, I wanted to do anything I could to get closer to the Lord and learn to love. The priest I went to for Confession also suggested that I go to the Adoration Chapel to pray. I was too embarrassed to tell him I didn't know what that was. However, I wanted to be obedient and do what he said, so I went.

I knew I still needed so much healing, and the process would take time. Being restored to who we truly are in Christ, knowing our identity, and being firmly rooted in it doesn't happen overnight.

The Adoration Chapel was in a tiny, modest room with only a few rows of chairs and kneelers on the back of them. A picture of Saint Padre Pio hung on the wall and a statue of Our Lady was in the corner. The people inside were quiet and so focused that they didn't even see me enter. It was clear to me that this was a place of prayer, and I closed my eyes and knelt quickly to pretend I knew what I was doing. Then, I sheepishly tried to open my right eye ever so slightly to look around at the others. They seemed like stone statues—no one moved or made a sound.

I completely overlooked the monstrance containing the Eucharist (consecrated host) that was front and center in the room. I guess in many ways, I remained so blind to how God was working in my life, but I felt like the whole room just stood still, and I was filled with peace.

On the way home, I thought, I need to do some research and find out more about it. I went online to find out what an Adoration Chapel was and felt so silly. Christ was right in front of me in the monstrance. His Body, Blood, Soul, and Divinity were present in the Eucharist. Truth, Beauty, and Goodness were right there!

"I am the bread of life. Your ancestors ate manna in the desert, but they died, this is the bread that comes down from heaven so that one may eat it and not die. I am the living bread that came down from heaven; whoever eats this bread will live forever; and the bread that I will give is my flesh for the life of the world."
—John 6:48–51

After learning this, I began to frequent Adoration and learned to sit in God's presence and rest in Him. I let Him love me as I offered Him my heart, and prayer became so much more than just going through the motions. I started honest one-on-one conversations with Him and surrendered my baggage, hurts, and wounds. As I came to know Him better, I also allowed Him to fill me with truth and love. Only then was I able to begin to bring His love into the world.

The more time I spent in Adoration, the fonder I became of it. I also immersed myself in key Scriptures about identity and love. And while I was beginning to learn that I was God's beloved daughter, I still didn't know in-depth who I really was and pondered, *What was I created for?*

Some days I sat in Adoration and asked Him repeatedly, "Who am I? Who do you say I am? Not what the world says I am. Who do you say I am?" We need to be persistent with that question, and some days I said, "Lord, I'm not leaving here until you tell me who I am." I would also ask Him to show me the lies in my heart that were blocking me from knowing the truth.

One day, I went with a pen and paper thinking maybe two or three lies would come to mind, and I would write them down. Instead, over eighty lies popped up, and the paper was so full I ran out of space! I began to glimpse the depth of my woundedness. So I continued going back several times a week, asking, "Who am I?"

Now, I'm not talking about a big, booming voice coming out of the sky. However, in silence, I was able to hear and recognize the thoughts that came to mind that seemed to fit in with what the Lord was telling me about myself.

After plenty of time in silence, it's easier to hear the small whisper in our hearts and the words of love that the Lord is hungry to speak to us. It could be like a thought in the heart, or maybe a song or Scripture comes to mind. Sometimes He also speaks through someone else who affirms us in our identity, or we get an email or text that answers our questions. His voice takes many forms, but He will answer us, and His answer will be consistent. It will also come with a peace and joy that heals our hearts.

He speaks to all of us in different ways according to our personality and how we will receive Him best, but He promises to guide us and be with us. He is constantly trying to communicate in some way and express His love and purpose for us. I realize now how many times He had spoken to me in my past and how I had doubted that it was Him or that He really cared about me.

Admittedly, I've shared some personal supernatural encounters in this book that many people may not experience and want to acknowledge that I didn't receive them because I'm special. It's just how God chose to speak to a very weak person like me. He does, however, speak to all of us in some way, shape, or form because He wants us to know Him and His love for us. He wants us to be happy in life by doing His will.

My grandma, the holiest woman I've ever known, said four Rosaries and the Divine Mercy Chaplet every day. Nonetheless, she had very few supernatural experiences. She walked in a beautiful, blind faith and kept her thoughts on God's truth and light. She lived simply and accepted all her circumstances to be from the hand of God. She was also very skilled at spiritual combat and wouldn't let any bad thoughts overcome her. She shut them down the moment they arrived and never left the presence of God. Grandma meditated on the Lord's goodness and believed blindly and boldly in Him. She stood firmly as His child.

Saint Teresa of Avila often spoke about her own weaknesses, and she felt that's why God had to communicate with her in such a unique way. She discusses in her books that it's not spiritual experiences that make a person holy, but rather how well they love. There is no other measure for holiness but love and virtue.

Furthermore, I've had people tell me that they wish for experiences like mine, but I tell them to be careful what they ask for. I'm a witness of God's mercy and rely on His grace with every breath. My encounter with Him wasn't just intended for me. It's also so I could share the good news with others. Being human and imperfect means constantly surrendering to the Lord, and He never fails to humble us when needed.

After my reversion, I continued to spend countless hours in adoration in the presence of the Lord. I needed to know I wasn't alone and that God was for me, so it didn't matter who was against me. I still was trying to find out who I was in Him, and honestly, there are many days when I go back to be reaffirmed.

It takes time for words of truth to sink in and for us to understand it, especially when we have been away from the Lord for so long. After we finally turn toward him, it takes time to believe we are all the amazing things He says we are. He tells us we're "beautiful, holy, pure, made new in Him, washed clean, and forgiven." No matter how He speaks to us, it takes hearing it repeatedly before we truly become rooted in it.

And I finally realized after years of working in the beauty industry that Adoration of the Blessed Sacrament, or intimate prayer with God, is the only true beauty treatment—the only one that's truly successful—because the soul is eternal. The beauty of our soul can grow as we create more room for God and let our egos shrink, as true beauty comes from the inside.

Since the fifth century BC, people have searched for the Fountain of Youth, and so much money and time have been wasted trying to find it. I've learned that being in the presence of the Lord is the only genuine "Fountain of Youth," as God lives in us and shines through us. Spending time in His presence increases our beauty and keeps us young at heart. As Saint Augustine said, "Love is the beauty of the soul."

It took me a long time to understand that I was truly beautiful in Him and that I'm a daughter of The King. To look in the mirror and into my own eyes and see Jesus is an ongoing effort, but that's what God desires. And we need to get to the place where we see Him in ourselves and others.

God sees our potential and He believes in us, yet we are usually the last to believe in ourselves. I think of the movie *The Lion King,*[6] when Simba's father died and he ran away for years. He thought it was all his fault and was living in shame. He only began to consider going home after seeing his reflection. Realizing he looked like his father and that his father was with him forever, he finally had the strength to return.

We all need inner strength to believe that we are walking in the power of Christ and that He can redeem and restore us. We are Children of The King. And once we can see our reflection in the light of Christ, there is no stopping what we can do. The enemy loses his power, and we become true disciples of Christ who lead others to Him.

After I experienced the illumination of my soul and turned back to the Lord, I had a clean slate and my life was blazing in a new way. I actually never intended to share my story publicly, and only told my family, friends, and spiritual director (a wonderful priest) what had happened. Then I spent over two years hiding in the pews and in volunteer ministry, rarely sharing my testimony with anyone.

Because of my past selfishness, I had also vowed to never go on stage or on camera again as I thought this was the honorable and humble thing to do. I couldn't see the beauty that would come from the ashes. But after nearly two years of prayer and healing, the Lord began to call me to speak and share my story.

He also eventually called me back into film and television for His glory. So I broke the vows I made because God was asking me to speak and share what was on His heart.

The process was all very organic, though not easy for me, and I was scared but accepted the invitations anyway. I wanted to be very careful that all honor and praise were given to God, because I'm aware that all I have is a gift, and He is the giver of gifts—apart from Him, we can do nothing. But in Him, all things are possible.

 PICKING UP THE PIECES

Have you ever asked the Lord who He says you are? Are you ready to spend time with Him in silence and be persistent in prayer? Do you believe He will answer you? Are you ready to know the truth and be set free? Plan a time to go to Adoration or spend time in quiet reflection and bring a pen and paper with you. Ask the Lord to bring to light the lies that you are holding in your heart and give them to Him. Also, take time when you look in the mirror to see Jesus in your eyes and remember that He lives in you and is with you. He will redeem, restore, and empower you to be you!

PRAYER

Lord Jesus, let me decrease so that you can increase. May your love shine through me onto others so that your beauty may be revealed. Help me to know the truth of who I am and to be deeply rooted in it so that I get my identity from you—not from what the world tells me. Please give me the grace to live in the world but not be of it. I love you and know that you love me more. Amen.

CHAPTER 22

COMMUNITY

And I tell you, ask and you will receive; seek and you will find;
knock and the door will be opened to you.
—Luke 11:9

My radical return to the Catholic Church and my new vigor in Christ seemed to shock many people who knew me before my reversion. I think they were curious about where things would lead. Some friends couldn't relate, because I had difficulty talking about makeup and other worldly things that used to dominate our conversations. For the first time in my life, I felt full and satisfied. Craving simplicity, I had no desire to even watch TV, and many years later, I rarely do. However, I enjoy films that have a good meaning behind them and those that are faith-based and inspirational. And, of course, I watch TV shows and movies with my kids when they want me to. Mostly now, I crave time in prayer and reading spiritually edifying books. I also love being with others in deep relationships.

I didn't disconnect from people but instead was forming healthier and more loving connections. How can you explain such a radical conversion? I felt like a stranger in the world—living in it but not of it. I was appreciating everything with a newfound beauty and desiring a more modest life.

As I began to spend more time at church, I also found myself participating in different ministries as I wanted to learn more and serve in any way I could. Hungering for truth and meaning, I felt a new fire raging in my heart. In addition to reading the Bible, I devoured the entire Catechism of the Catholic Church.

And, in my thirst for knowledge, I also stumbled upon a website about Saint Teresa of Avila. She was a zealous and brave Carmelite nun with a vibrant personality. As I read her book *Interior Castle,* [7] it felt like she was speaking the same language as me. She described things similar to what I was experiencing but were often difficult to verbalize. In no way am I comparing myself to her, but it was a delight to have someone who made me feel understood.

Saint Teresa of Avila's humility so moved me that I decided to make her my patron saint. She realized all her strength came from God and relied on Him for everything. Even trials she viewed as blessings and saw God's hand at work.

During this time, I thought I felt a call to be a Carmelite nun like her. However, that didn't make sense for someone like me with children, so I knew it couldn't be God's will. He will never ask us to do something that goes against our vocation.

Then, miraculously, I found out that there was an event about prayer through OCDS (The Secular Order of Discalced Carmelites) called "How Does Your Garden Grow?" The nuns of the Discalced Carmelites, such as Saint Teresa of Avila and Saint Therese of Lisieux, are cloistered. The friars live in a monastery but travel to teach and share the Gospel. I had never heard of OCDS but learned this secular order consists of laypeople out in the world helping others. They meet in community monthly and are approved as part of The Roman Catholic Church.

I decided to go to the event to check it out, but when I got there, my head immediately began spinning and the walls seemed to be closing in on me. They were doing different workshops on prayer, and confusion and a strong sense of unworthiness began to overtake me. I worried I wouldn't understand what they were saying because I wasn't sure if I fit in or if I even knew how to pray—I assumed everyone there was "holier" than me. And I contemplated bolting out the door, because despite having spent much time in prayer, I still felt inadequate.

Without realizing it, what I was experiencing was a spiritual attack. I still needed stronger roots in the Word of God to claim my true identity. When we have these moments, we must become aware that they are not from God. The enemy doesn't want us to be part of anything that helps us grow in our faith, and he uses these tactics to try to push us off course.

Luckily, in this moment, I met a friar and began telling him my fears. He asked me to stay and ignore my insecurities, and I'm so glad I did. After the talks and by the end of the day, I felt like I belonged and knew God wanted me to be there.

That special event turned into the beginning of a three-year discernment to join the community. The Carmelite order is gifted with grace-filled prayer for the church and others. The meetings I attended opened with thirty minutes of silence contemplating the love of God and His presence within. Then we got into formation groups, discussed books on the lives of saints, and helped each other grow in knowledge and virtue by sharing life experiences.

It's beautiful to be part of a community where you feel loved and accepted. And after three years of formation, I made my first (temporary) promises of poverty, chastity, and obedience per my state in life. For example, taking a vow of poverty in the secular world doesn't mean you can't have money, but rather, that you should have a spirit of detachment from it. Chastity is about pure, unconditional love, and if married, you can still be intimate with your spouse while at the same time having a chaste heart. The promise for obedience means surrendering to God's will and the church teachings.

The day of my first promises was extraordinary. Filled with such elation, I could feel my face beaming with happiness. And without a doubt, my time with the Carmelites brought me great healing through experiencing a place where everyone was focused on receiving God's love in order to give it.

I also learned to pray for others and not just myself. When we begin to face outward and can be present to others in their needs, we begin to walk with Christ. Above all, that's what I was seeking.

Additionally, seeing the different personalities and gifts within the people there was like spending time in a garden full of unique flowers. None was as the other. Saint Therese of Lisieux considered herself God's little flower, doing little things with love for His glory. She shared how all the flowers are needed to make up the body of Christ: "I understood how all the flowers God created are beautiful—how the splendor of the rose and the whiteness of the lily do not take away from the perfume of the violet or the simplicity of the daisy. I understood that if all flowers wanted to be roses, nature would lose her springtime beauty, and the fields would no longer be decked out with the wildflower. And so it is in the world of souls . . . Jesus's garden. He willed to create souls comparable to lilies and roses, but he created small ones as well . . . and these must be content to be daisies or violets destined to give joy to God's glances, when he looks down at His feet. Perfection consists in doing God's will . . . in being what He would have us be."

When we start to appreciate the differences in one another and see the goodness we were created for, Jesus's garden becomes more fragrant. We are all human with fragile hearts and weaknesses, but when we come together for the sake of Love, wonderful things happen.

I also used to have an idea in my head that the closer we are to God, the less we need Him, but the opposite is true. The more illuminated our souls become, the more we see that we are incredibly weak on our own, and that all the good in us is God Himself.

He makes us strong and uses us despite our weaknesses, if we turn to Him for strength. The spiritual life is full of paradoxes—in our weakness, we are strong, and in losing our lives, we gain them.

"For whoever wishes to save his life will lose it, but whoever loses his life for my sake will save it."

—Luke 9:24

The more we surrender our lives to God, the more we can live and love freely. How can we put our relationship with Christ into action and help others? Prayer is one thing we can all do for each other as an act of love. How easy is it to see someone in need, even a stranger, and offer to pray for them? Or even just let them know we notice them and care? The fruits of our prayer life should lead to this, and if it doesn't, then it's safe to say we aren't praying at all.

Sometimes we overcomplicate what prayer even is. Saint Teresa of Avila said, "Mental prayer in my opinion is nothing else than an intimate sharing between friends; it means taking time frequently to be alone with Him who we know loves us." Prayer should lead us to lovingly help our neighbor. And our safety net of knowing if we truly have intimacy with God is to examine whether we love others and are bearing good fruit.

"Just so, every good tree bears good fruit, and a rotten tree bears bad fruit. A good tree cannot bear bad fruit, nor can a rotten tree bear good fruit."
—Matthew 7:17–18

Despite my ongoing insecurities and battles, I couldn't doubt that the fruit in my life was in fact good and that the Lord was leading me. I now realize that sometimes God puts us in places for a particular time to teach us and prepare us for what's coming next. During my years with OCDS, I experienced layer after layer of healing love. I grew in my confidence in Christ, and my fears began to subside.

When I first started attending meetings, I was super quiet and still very broken. I felt like a shipwreck victim who had stumbled ashore not knowing where they belonged. In the end, I came away healed, secure in my identity, and ready to share the Gospel with the world.

Then the Lord began calling me to more speaking engagements and ministry endeavors. Because of this, I couldn't make the monthly meetings anymore, but if it's God's will, I will return someday. However, I don't doubt I was sent there for a time and reason. I wouldn't be able to fulfill the ministry and mission I have today without having learned through OCDS to sit still, pray, and love deeply.

I also can't tell you how many times I still reach for my Carmelite saint books during a spiritual battle so I can see clearly again. As Saint Teresa of Avila said, "Let nothing disturb you, let nothing frighten you, all things are passing away; God never changes. Patience obtains all things. Whoever has God lacks nothing; God alone suffices." A new perspective like this often helps me persevere. Scriptures and advice from saints fill us with truth and give us strength in times of need.

The Catholic Church has several different religious orders, such as the Carmelites, Franciscans, Dominicans, and Benedictines. It's something to discern if you feel the tug in your heart toward one of them. Going to an event and reading books written by a saint in that order would be a great start. You can also find other ways to become more involved in your church in general by researching different ministries to see if your heart feels called to a new opportunity. The Holy Spirit will always guide us.

 PICKING UP THE PIECES

Is God calling you to any religious lay orders or ministries? How have doubt and fear tried to stop you from doing something God was calling you to? Have you ever discerned a call to religious life? Are there any community or church events tugging on your heart to attend? Do you have a favorite saint? Remember to ask them to intercede for you daily and know you are never alone on this journey.

PRAYER

Lord Jesus, help me to see your hand in all things. Please help me to understand my calling in life and to have clarity on the path to holiness. Saint Teresa of Avila, pray for us! Amen.

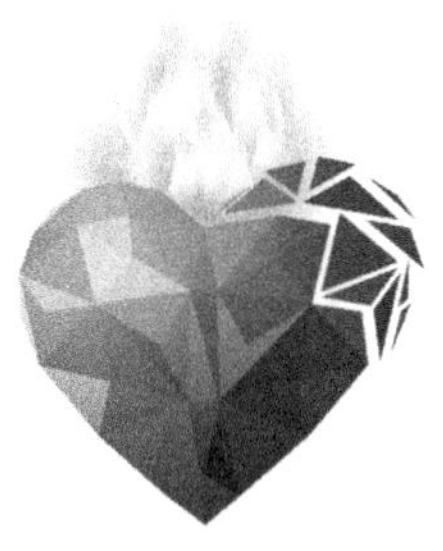

CHAPTER 23

USING YOUR GIFTS

I say I will not mention him, I will no longer speak in his name.
But then it is as if fire is burning in my heart, imprisoned in my
bones; I grow weary holding back, I cannot!
—Jeremiah 20:9

During my time with the Carmelites, I reflected on where the Lord was leading me. Soon, I felt called to leave the cosmetic company as I had completely lost my passion for putting makeup on people. I wanted to tell them that their problem in life wasn't that they didn't know how to apply their eyeliner. The problem was much deeper, as many like me struggled with poor self-image and didn't know their true beauty and worth. It was also becoming increasingly painful for me to sell the products and attend company events with my eyes wide open, as the Holy Spirit was tugging my heart in a new direction.

I started "preaching" more than speaking at events, and the focus of my talks quickly became more about inner beauty than artistry or products. I remember someone saying to me, "What are you doing? Are you trying to sell makeup or God? What did your talk have to do with makeup? What's going on?" Others told me they were inspired by my words and bought the makeup anyway.

The discernment on whether or not to stay in the cosmetic business was a long process, because I was still learning to discern God's will, and it took me three-and-a-half painful years to resign. However, during that time, I had already started volunteering in various ministries and had begun publicly sharing my story too. Providentially, for the previous six years through the company, I had been able to work with teens at a children's shelter. Although it was under the guise of teaching them how to do their makeup for interviews, I began to incorporate God into the messaging.

The shelter was well organized, sparkling clean, and charming. The grounds were filled with colorful flowers and greenery. It was obvious from a visual perspective that the people running it wanted to create a safe and welcoming environment for those living there, and the staff that I encountered had hearts on fire for the youth. They were concerned with their well-being, and you could see they loved them very much.

I always prayed on my way there, for the teens' hearts to be open to whatever the Lord wanted to say to them through me. I knew they had been through some very rough times, and many felt unknown. Images of a good family were often shattered. Also, several of them had not been exposed to religion or had given up on God, projecting life's hurtful experiences on Him. The stories they shared with me were heartbreaking, yet I could feel God's love for them, and I sensed He wanted to penetrate their hearts with the truth that He's a good Father.

On one specific day, I felt called to bring a copy of Saint Mother Teresa's "I Thirst" prayer with me to the shelter, but my printer at home had stopped working just before I left, so I didn't have many copies. I thought, *Oh well, I doubt any of them would want it anyway.* However, when I got there, they began fighting over the prayer, and we ran out quickly.

There happened to be a copier in the room where I was doing the presentation, and a staff member told me we were in the only room in the entire building that even had one. God provided! We could print more of the prayers, and I was astonished at how hungry the teens were for Jesus.

Every time I drove home from there, I'd be smiling from ear to ear and feeling like I was floating up in the clouds. I now realize God was pointing out that He was calling me to serve Him, not the cosmetic company. And with my return to the church, an authentic relationship with the Lord, and spiritual direction, I began to understand things better.

I chose to resign and willingly walked away from most of my life's savings, which had been invested in the cosmetic company. I gave away all of my shares—accounting for 70 percent ownership—because I knew God was calling me into full-time ministry.

It was also a burden to keep everything running when my heart wasn't in it and was actually very freeing to leave. What might have seemed like a heavy and challenging decision felt so right and light. What God had in store was and continues to be much more than I could have ever imagined. Our peace, contentment, and passion are in doing His will, and nothing else will ever satisfy.

That said, I can't say my decision to leave was altogether popular. Many couldn't understand how I went from being so worldly to wanting to serve God. I also found out that someone went around and said terrible things about me. Then, I heard from others that people I considered friends had agreed. They had no idea how much pain and suffering they caused. However, God saw it all and never left my side. And as I gave these wounds to Him, He cleansed and healed them with His own tears. They were no longer hurting me but the One within me. What they sowed to try to harm me only brought me blessing instead.

"Therefore, I am content with weaknesses, insults, hardships,
persecutions, and constraints, for the sake of Christ, for when
I am weak, then I am strong."
—2 Corinthians 12:10

During this time, I leaned on the Beatitudes and in particular Matthew 5:10: "Blessed are they that are persecuted for the sake of righteousness, for theirs is the kingdom of heaven." I can't say that I felt blessed. It was more that I was now aware that my true treasure would be in heaven.

The Gospel isn't about God using the perfect. Rather, He restores and heals the wounded. Then He directs their lives to truth and purpose.

As God healed me and helped me let go of worldly things that were keeping me from growing in holiness, I began to gain more trust in Him and His provisions. The more I acknowledged that I didn't deserve it, the more graces He gave. He doesn't give us what we deserve, but rather what He knows we need, and He's a generous giver. Others may have questioned my decisions, but I know I found the pearl of great price.

"Again, the kingdom of heaven is like a merchant searching for fine pearls. When he finds a pearl of great price, he goes and sells all that he has and buys it."
—*Matthew 13:45–46*

Over time, ironically, many of those who had opposed me saw the fruits of God's work and became supporters of the ministry. Eventually, one of the people who hurt me the most actually reached out to me with a prayer request in a time of need. It certainly was a redeeming moment, given all they had done against me. I had already forgiven them and never stopped praying for their conversion, so I rejoiced when God answered my prayer.

"Father, forgive them, they know not what they do."
—*Luke 23:34*

Our peace comes from doing God's will, and it's not always easy to end something, especially when others oppose us. But it's true that when we close a door to something that's not God's desire for us, He opens a new door in His time. Our lives and happiness are a big deal to Him, and He won't disappoint us. He has something so much better planned, even when we can't see it yet or understand how it will happen.

When we are headed in the right direction and our wills are aligned with His, we will be consoled and filled with peace, hope, faith, love, and joy. We will have the energy and excitement to move in that direction. As long as we are living a righteous life, our inner compass will always guide us in which way to go.

The enemy will try to entice us in the opposite direction and tempt us to give up. He will try to make us think we're not equipped or that something is wrong with us. So we must be aware of this, resist these attempts, and keep moving forward.

The truth is that because the Holy Spirit lives in us, deep down we already know the answers but often we don't trust God enough. Or we can be afraid of how difficult the sacrifices will be to make a change. However, if we choose to accept God's will, He will give us the grace, strength, and everything we need to succeed. Seeking Him, trusting in Him, and remaining firm in our choices are key.

> ♡ PICKING UP THE PIECES
>
> Have you ever been a part of something you knew God didn't want you to do anymore? How did you get out of it? How did you feel after you made the change? Are you currently discerning God's will in an area of your life and unsure of what to do? Have you experienced opposition in a choice you made to serve God?

PRAYER

Lord Jesus, please help me know your will for my life. Please guide me, strengthen me, and provide for me. Thank you for always wanting the best for me and having such amazing plans. I love you. Amen.

CHAPTER 24

EVANGELISM

Then I heard the voice of the Lord saying,
"Whom shall I send? Who will go for us?"
"Here I am," I said; "send me!"
—Isaiah 6:8

After I left the company for full-time ministry, I faced a significant problem. I didn't know yet what that ministry was, and now I needed a job. It was a time of trial, prayer, and deep trust. The waiting seemed like an eternity, but my time with the Carmelites helped prepare me for this transition.

I learned to sit still in the presence of God and let Him love me so that I could begin to love others. Having been selfish for so many years, I desired to open my heart to becoming more selfless. It's a battle every day, but we must continue fighting as our human nature and tug toward sin tend to lead us to focus on ourselves. However, Jesus shows us that true love faces outward and gives of oneself. So I took a leap of faith and dove in, although I still suffered many moments of doubt and fear.

At this point, I had spent a few years in volunteer ministry and had already begun sharing my story at events. And at my home parish, I was the spiritual chair of a mom's group and also helped facilitate an evangelization program. Additionally, I reflected on how close I felt to God when I spoke to the teens at the children's shelter and how transformed my heart would feel on the way home. I also remembered being unable to sleep the night before speaking at a youth event because I was so excited. It just seemed right, and someone who saw me afterward said I was glowing. They had never seen me so happy before and were amazed at how full of life I was.

As these desires continued to grow, I told someone very close to me that I felt a possible call to be a youth minister. Then I quickly worked on putting my résumé together. When I asked them to look it over and give me advice, they took it and threw it at me. They said, "No one will ever hire you as a youth minister. You have no experience."

I can still see the résumé floating in the air, headed toward me and slowly drifting to the ground—dragging my heart with it. I was crushed. I had already applied for another youth minister position before redoing my résumé and had gotten a "don't call us, we'll call you" response. Yet I still had hope and could feel the calling inside.

I love the Mother Angelica quote, "Unless you are willing to do the ridiculous, God will not do the miraculous. When you have God, you don't have to know everything about it; you just do it."

That night, at 10:00 p.m., I frantically called my spiritual director and told him what had happened. With hurt and confusion in my voice, I said, "Father, it's in my prayer that I'm supposed to be a youth minister. I'm not sure why, and it's true I don't have much experience. But what do you think of this? What should I do? What's the next step?" He tried to calm me down and said, "Joelle, if it's God's will, it will happen. Trust in God and get some rest."

The next day I felt compelled to go to a different church for daily Mass. It was beautiful with stunning architecture and had arched ceilings with wooden beams, incredible statues of the saints, and gorgeous stained-glass windows. I saw a fellow Carmelite lay sister there, and I went up to her after Mass to say hello. Then I asked if she could help me put together a better youth minister résumé, because I knew she was an intelligent woman.

Her eyes opened wide and she said, "Wow, you're not going to believe this, but our youth minister just put in his notice and is going to leave. It hasn't even been announced yet." I thought right away, *Oh, that's it. I have a job. It's mine! This is where I'm supposed to be!* I was convinced that this was Divine Providence.

She said, "Well, I'll bring you into the office to introduce you to the pastor." However, he wouldn't see me as he was swamped with work and said sternly, "Tell her to send in her résumé."

I started to cry as I thought, *Oh, I thought you wanted me to do this, Lord, and he won't even see me.* But I sent in my résumé anyway, and the church proceeded to post the job at the diocese. They interviewed many people, and at this point, I wondered if it was truly what God wanted me to do. I had felt so strongly called to this, but the waiting seemed like forever, even though it was only a few months.

Finally, one day I prayed, "Lord, I thought this is where you were you wanted me. Can you put an urgency in the priest's heart and have him call me and let me know what's going on? If I'm supposed to be the youth minister at this parish, can you let him know too?"

Right after that prayer, I decided, *You know what, I'm going to email the priest and check in with him to see where they are in the process of hiring.* At the very same time I was emailing him, he called me and left a voice message that they wanted me to come in for a second interview. Then, he saw my email and wrote back that he had just left me a voice mail while I was writing to him. At that moment, I knew God was with us. I still had to go through the process and heard they interviewed many people for the position of Director of High School Youth Ministry. But by the power of the Holy Spirit, God's will was done, and I was hired!

When you feel something so deeply in your heart, you can't go by what others say. Think of David and Goliath. David was so much smaller and wasn't as experienced in battle, but he worked according to his strengths. He knew God was with him and confidently won the fight. When God calls us to do something, nothing and no one can stop it other than ourselves. The enemy will do his best to try to get us to turn around. He will try to convince us that we aren't good enough or experienced enough. However, we are made in the image of God, and God IS, so we ARE. We are enough, and He doesn't put deep desires in our hearts that He doesn't want to fulfill.

Part of our spiritual armor is the belt of truth—God's Word. We need to plant it in our heart and trust our gut, and we can't let doubt get in the way.

God wants us to trust with abandon, and if something isn't meant to be, then it won't happen. However, we won't know unless we try. After my encounter with the Lord, I'm deathly afraid to die and have Him say that He put people and opportunities in my life to help build His Kingdom, but I didn't believe enough to ask for help or say yes. Sometimes, even when things seem impossible, we just have to trust the Lord and go for it—so I did.

♡ PICKING UP THE PIECES

Have you ever felt called to something but were scared to do it? Have you ever had someone else tell you that you couldn't do something even though you knew it felt right inside? Have you ever waited to hear back from someone, and it seemed like forever, and you began to fear the worst? Have you remembered to ask God to guide you and all those involved to do His will?

PRAYER

Lord Jesus, please help us to trust in you and follow the prompts of the Holy Spirit. Please open the doors that need to be opened in our lives and close the doors that need to be closed. You know what is best for us. Help us to hear your voice and persevere even when others try to make us doubt. Please take away any fear of the future as we freely choose to place it in your loving hands. Amen.

CHAPTER 25

USING YOUR HURTS

But he was pierced for our sins, crushed for our iniquity.
He bore the punishment that makes us whole,
by his wounds we were healed.
—Isaiah 53:5

Before beginning the youth ministry position, I decided to go on a retreat at a convent for a few days to spend some time in silence. I had never been to one before and didn't know what to expect. When I arrived, I was delighted to see the grounds, which featured a pretty pond with paths and benches surrounding it. The birds were singing sweetly and the air was crisp and fresh. My room was immaculate, and to my surprise, when I hopped onto the bed it was very comfortable. The coverlet was adorned with tiny pink roses, and I felt like a princess. I was told the nuns' beds weren't as lavish as the guest rooms.

Astonishingly, I felt at home there, and it was good for me to take some time away to contemplate what was going on. However, I continued to also have moments of uncertainty. It still seemed surreal to me that I, of all people, was at a convent and had experienced such a dramatic return to Christ.

I know others thought it was strange that an actress/model/CEO was becoming a youth minister. Honestly, I did, too, but I just felt in my heart that it was the next step toward wherever God was leading. However, I had no idea how He would eventually resurrect my other passions for His glory as well. Over time God would reveal, heal, and send me to where I was supposed to be. This period of purification and service was a great blessing, because I was finally doing something for others and not thinking of myself.

When people reminded me of my past accomplishments, it seemed to me as if they were talking about someone else. I knew I had done these things, but the memories seemed so vague and distant. The new person I was becoming didn't care about worldly status anymore, and I thank God for this great grace as I was given the opportunity to begin walking in complete faith.

At the convent, I wanted to spend time praying about the theme for the ministry that year and be open to anything the Lord wanted to share with me. The only instance in which I broke silence was to speak daily to a nun for spiritual direction. Sister Francesca was so compassionate and gentle, and the Holy Spirit spoke eloquently through her. Angelic-looking with skin that glowed, she had a special way of explaining things with a kind smile and sparkle in her eyes. It brought me so much peace to just be in her presence.

On the first day there, when I went to spiritual direction, I shared my story. I said, "I just don't understand why God would use someone like me, who has done all these things, and who has messed up so badly. I know He has called me to ministry, but why?" And she said, "Have you ever heard of the phrase, the 'wounded healer'? You are a wounded healer. God is healing your wounds and using you to bring healing to others." I was intrigued and surprised by her answer as I had never heard that phrase before, and I left the session still trying to understand what it meant.

Next, I walked down the long corridor and spent time in the chapel praying in front of the Tabernacle (a locked box that holds the Eucharist after Mass). I was there alone for many hours, and at one point, I felt the Holy Spirit prompt me to go to the library down the hall. On my way there, I noticed glorious artwork on the walls, and without realizing it, the Lord was preparing my heart for what was about to happen.

As I walked into the library, I immediately saw on the wall a striking picture of the face of Jesus. It was a mosaic, and inside the pieces were people of all different races, ages, and social statuses. I froze and paused to stare at it, trying to comprehend what it meant. Then, after a few minutes, I moved on and began to look for a book to read. As I wandered among the bookshelves, I prayed, "Lord, what books should I read? I want to know what your plans are for me and how you want to use me?"

The library had literally around a thousand to choose from, but one stood out, and I felt prompted to take it off the shelf. The title was *Called to Heal: Releasing the Transforming Power of God,*[8] by Fr. Ralph A. DiOrio. As I opened the book, the first thing I did was look at the table of contents. One of the chapters listed was called "The Wounded Healer." I thought, *Wow. That's the second time today that I've heard that phrase,* and I shut the book in complete awe with tears streaming down my face. Then I turned it over to read more about it. On the back cover was the same image of Jesus I had just been pondering in the mosaic picture on the wall. My jaw dropped even further as I thought, *What are the chances that out of nearly a thousand books here, I would choose this very one with this image on it?*

The picture had the following inscription written below it: "We are all one in Christ. Hurting one, we hurt all. Helping one, we help all. Heal us and bring us together, oh God."

God had just given me my calling—one meant for all of us. We're called to heal, and we're called to love. We're called to be wounded healers, and it's love that heals. None of us have gone through life unscathed. And once we allow Christ's love to heal and fill our wounds, we can become more sympathetic toward others who are hurting.

We know what it feels like to be wounded, and it comforts those suffering to see someone who has made it through. It brings hope and light to the darkness as we're all one in Christ. Jesus is our Master, and we are all one in His heart. It is He who heals us and brings us together. He helps us pick up the pieces of our lives to become wounded healers and love one another in Him.

As a little girl, I was always very sensitive and would often cry and say, "You hurt my feelings." A family member would laugh at me for this, which only increased my pain. But I now realize that even something like sensitivity, which can sometimes be a cross, can also be a gift.

In ministry and acting, being empathetic helps one better understand what others are going through. Being a wounded healer isn't about worthiness. It's about mission. It's about being the hands and feet of Jesus. He died to save us and make us whole again.

"By His wounds, we were healed."
—Isaiah 53:5

As true disciples of Christ, we share in His compassion for what others are going through and are moved to be there for one another. But we need to take time to hear God in silence, and a retreat is a great beginning. He never disappoints us and is always present.

Being persistent in prayer and growing in trust is critical. Once we genuinely seek God's will, doors begin to open. He has promised us that He has a plan and purpose for our lives, and we're all called to heal. As Henri J.M. Nouwen said, "When our wounds cease to be a source of shame, and become a source of healing, we have become wounded healers."

I often envision Jesus after the resurrection, walking around with His wounds visible. I believe that regardless if they were seen by the naked eye, rays of light were shining through the holes in His hands and the places He was pierced. He was not walking in brokenness but rather in strength and glory. His wounds became a reminder of His journey of Love, and His Love continued to pour out through them.

When we surrender our lives and memories to the Lord, He heals our hearts and we begin to walk in His power. It's much greater than worldly power because it emanates from the love of Jesus's most Sacred Heart, which conquers all. And as the Lord puts our broken pieces back together, His light begins to shine through the mosaic Masterpiece He has created. Our new image doesn't deny our past, but rather embraces it for His glory.

There would be no healing without a wound. And while the Lord may not heal every wound in the way that we would like Him to, His light still illuminates those places and shines through us onto others.

"You are the light of the world. A city set on a mountain cannot be hidden. Nor do they light a lamp and then put it under a bushel basket; it is set on a lampstand, where it gives light to all in the house. Just so your light must shine before others, that they may see your good deeds and glorify your heavenly Father."
—Matthew 5:16

♡ PICKING UP THE PIECES

How can we use our past wounds to become wounded healers? Spend time in prayer, asking the Lord to reveal your wounds and allowing Him to enter into your woundedness to fill you with His truth and love. Take time to see what gifts, talents, and graces you've been given. Let God decide how to use your gifts and talents to bring healing to others. Follow the prompts of the Holy Spirit daily and go where He tells you to go. Be God's light in the world!

PRAYER

Lord Jesus, please heal us in any way that is needed so we can bring your healing love to others and serve you. Thank you for speaking to us through others and circumstances. Help us to be wounded healers who bring your light into the world. Amen.

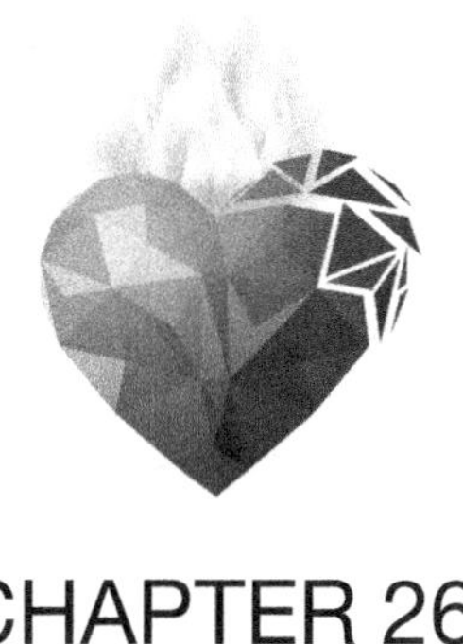

CHAPTER 26

IDENTITY IN CHRIST

*The gatekeeper opens it for him, and the sheep
hear his voice, as he calls his own sheep by name
and leads them out.*
—John 10:3

I began youth ministry with a great burst of excitement and planned a big welcome luau for the kids and their parents. Hundreds of people showed up wearing vibrant colors, and of course, I had flower leis for everyone. The year's theme that came to me during my time at the convent was "One Love, One Life," and our focus was on building a relationship with Jesus. It was centered on the fact that life is short, and He's the only one that satisfies the deepest longing in our hearts.

The parish had already gone through several youth ministers before I arrived, and many of the people who first greeted me wanted to know how long I would stay. I was sincere in telling them from the beginning that God had called me there, but I didn't know for how long. It could be one year, two years, three years, or ten years, but I would have to go where He wanted when it was time.

From the day I arrived, I had an intuitive feeling that the Lord would use me to grow the ministry. He was also teaching me many things that would become a strong foundation for my future work, and I had an awareness He was forming me for whatever was next.

Ironically, God also used my past business experience when it came time to develop a team and plan a three-year curriculum. And although it was very intense getting the ministry up and running, I was thankful to have terrific volunteers. They gave so much of themselves to help, and each of them had different gifts. I witnessed how God can do mighty things through us when we come together for His purpose.

During my time at the parish, I met wonderful people and observed up-close what young people are suffering through these days. It made me think of my past, and as the Lord used me to heal others, He continued to heal me through them. Memories of my teenage years, especially those I was inspired to share in this book, came to the surface and became purified. Because of this, I was able to minister with sympathy, while bringing hope and healing to broken hearts.

On Sunday evenings, during our faith formation gathering, I often spoke and presented a topic. I noticed it was in these moments that I felt incredibly alive—I looked forward to those talks all week. In addition, many people came in for prayer during the week, and I realized how my years in various ministries had helped prepare me for this. We also took the teens to several conferences and saw them experience major spiritual transformations.

Whenever I listened to other speakers presenting, I felt an extraordinary desire and knowing in my heart that God wanted me to speak for Him at events like these too. I was already being invited to speak at other places when I wasn't working at the parish but wasn't publicizing my speaking ministry. It was just happening, and I didn't understand why. If I'm honest, I was scared to even know.

I think we're often more scared of what God might actually do with us if we said "yes." We always have excuses for why we can't do things, such as "I'm not good enough," "I'm not young or old enough," "I'm not experienced enough," and so on.

Simultaneously, the Lord also started to resurrect the love of acting in my heart. At one point, I was asked to dress up and act as Saint Therese for the parish's preschoolers. It reignited the flame in my heart, and I experienced a sense of profound peace and joy in playing the role.

On another occasion, when I was in my office praying about acting and how much I missed it, a parishioner came in to tell me about a Christian film her friend was producing. She also asked me to play a role in a scene they were preparing for a parish activity. These little "God-wink" moments continued to lead to more roles and opened doors down the road.

Additionally, the teens at the parish knew that I was a huge advocate of retreats, and indeed I encouraged them to attend as many as possible. And since it's important to practice what you preach, when I found out that the parish was holding an adult retreat, I decided to check it out.

I knew from experience that every time we go on a retreat, God has something special in store for every single person there. It's so important to take time out of our busy lives to get away and grow in a relationship with Him. That way, we can clearly hear about the things He wants us to work on so we can be healed more deeply and serve faithfully.

When I got to the retreat, I didn't know many people and felt a bit uncomfortable. We began in a dimly lit room with chairs arranged in a circle and soft music playing in the background. The leaders gave everyone a candle, then asked us to stand and say our names. I had already come very far in being healed, as holding the candle and seeing the flames no longer triggered bad memories of the fire.

My eyes were now on Christ, and my past was being redeemed. However, getting up and saying my name in front of people was more embarrassing than you can imagine. People think that I'm an extreme extrovert because I talk in front of large crowds and approach strangers with messages of God's love. My public speaking skills are certainly a gift from God, and I love interacting with people. However, getting up and saying my name in front of a group like this was not easy for me.

I was full of dread as my turn got closer, but I couldn't leave the circle at this point. When I got up to say my name, I said it with a question mark. I was like, "Joelle?" Right away, the Holy

Spirit highlighted that for me. Then I sat down and realized that after all those years of going to Adoration and asking God who I am, I still said my name with a question mark. I began to understand that we're never done growing in our identity and spent the entire retreat asking the Lord once again, "Who am I?"

That weekend, everyone on the host team got up and gave their witnesses. As they shared their stories, I began to see myself in them, and certain details made me think, *Oh, that seems like part of me and my journey. That fits.* God showed me that He was in them, that He was in me, and that we're all connected in Him.

As the witnesses spoke, I wrote down words about them that I also saw in myself: *Mom, Beloved Daughter, Chosen, Redeemed, Forgiven, Healed, Survivor, Strong, Peacemaker, Joyful, Unique, Adventurous, and Worthy,* to name a few.

After the retreat, I took all the words I had written down and put them on my closet wall, which I called my prayer wall. I'd seen a film where a woman posted Scriptures in her closet to help her pray and "fight the good fight." And I loved the idea of putting Scriptures in a visible place to help me with my battles as I was determined not just to know who I was but also to never forget.

We all face different struggles, but the Scriptures can speak to our areas of weakness and woundedness. They can replace lies with the ultimate truth. After some time, I found that I had memorized the verses and didn't even need to look at my prayer wall that often anymore. God's words had become one with my heart.

I also posted photos of good memories on this wall, like a picture of the *Called to Heal* book, which helped me remember what my mission was. These things reminded me that even when God feels far away, He always comes through in times of weakness.

He does have a plan for us, and His love never fails. I have since put the things on my prayer wall in an album that I look through from time to time to recall how good and faithful the Lord is.

Additionally, while at the retreat, we got to sleep in the church, and I chose the spot just under the Tabernacle. Without realizing it, I slept soundly through the entire night, with more than fifty candles surrounding me. My fear of fire was long gone, and the fire within my heart was growing stronger and stronger. I had the living flame of love within and treasured that peaceful night. I felt like I belonged and knew I was a child of God in my Father's house.

Our true identity is in God, and He is Love and lives within us. The good things in us are who we are because we are made in His image. That day at the retreat, I learned the meaning of my name and your name as I began to see Christ more clearly in us. True love sees Christ in each other.

Although we have all been through things in life that have chipped away at our identity, God our Father wants us to know who we really are and that we belong to Him. Once we can open our hearts and wounds to His love, we will then be filled with strength to walk securely toward our future. The Holy Spirit will animate our lives and lead us to the next steps we need to take. May we all get to the place where we can say our names with confidence in Him and stay rooted and grounded in His truth for good.

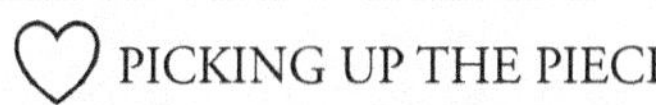

PICKING UP THE PIECES

Have you ever had to get up in front of someone and say your name? How did you feel? Have you ever questioned who you are and why you're here? Are you able to see Christ in yourself and others? Consider starting a prayer wall in your home or putting together an album where you can put Scriptures that have touched your heart and photos of "God-incidences."

PRAYER

Lord Jesus, help me to know the true meaning of my name and to say it with confidence. Please help me to know my worth and to see you in others. May we all be united in your love and feel safe in your most Sacred Heart. Amen.

LISTENING TO THE HOLY SPIRIT

This is my commandment:
love one another as I love you.
—John 15:12

With my new identity in Christ and as I allowed God to guide my life, nothing surprised me anymore. While we often limit what God can do in our lives, I was finally open and expectant to see Him at work all around me.

The year after the retreat, I took a trip to Florida to visit my favorite private beach there and spend time in prayer. It's a true paradise where the water is a bright turquoise and the palm trees sway in the wind. Nothing beats having your toes in the warm sand and looking out at the vast ocean. It creates an awareness of how small we are and provides a glimpse of how big God is. Even the power of the waves is mesmerizing, and it's easy to get carried away in currents of grace while contemplating His majesty.

While there, I like to take long walks and talk with the Lord. Usually, I bring my Bible and some spiritual reading as well. But as soon as I got to the beach this time and sat down to relax, I noticed my phone stopped working. Immediately, it came to mind how a few weeks prior, the same thing had happened. I had taken it to a national phone retailer near where I lived, but once I got to the store, the phone worked just fine. In the process, I ended up having a beautiful encounter with someone there who the Lord put in my path. So my first question on the beach was, "Is there someone at the store here in Florida that you want me to meet, Lord?" I didn't hear anything back, but I thought to myself, *I better go check this out, and if my phone starts working when I get there, I'll know.*

I found the closest phone store and walked in. Open to whatever might happen next, I met a young, handsome employee who took my phone and quickly turned it on. He said, "Ma'am, your phone works fine," in a sweet and curious voice. Of course, I had tried fifty different times, and it wouldn't work for me. So I knew at that moment that the Lord had sent me, and I quickly found a way to bring God into our conversation.

I thanked him and began to tell him that I had come to the beach to pray. I briefly shared some of my reversion story with him, and then he revealed that his dad was a priest. He said, "My father is a Lutheran priest, and he wants to become Roman Catholic, but he's still discerning. To be honest, I think I'm a big disappointment to him. My heart is far from God, and I know I'm not doing what I should."

I told him that God loves him, is calling him closer, and that I felt I was sent there to meet him and share this. His eyes filled up with tears. It was such a simple message, but hearing it from a total stranger touched his heart. It's as if he had given up and thought God wouldn't love him or that he was too far gone to be reached.

The Lord was very present with us as we spoke. Then this guy looked at me as he held back his tears and said words that pierced my heart. He said, "Who are you? What is your calling?" He couldn't deny that God was with us, and he wanted to know how I had known to go to the store that day. What I said to him was the very thing that he needed to hear at that moment. I looked at him and smiled as the words that surprisingly flowed out of my mouth were, "You. You are my calling."

Saint Therese spent years trying to find her vocation and her calling. Even though she had become a nun and submitted her life to the Lord, it bothered her that she didn't know what her specific purpose was within her vocation. Finally, she figured it out one day and exclaimed, "At last, I have found my vocation. In the heart of the Church, I will be Love."

What if our calling is just that simple? What if our calling is to love the person that's right in front of us? What if we remain open to seeing God in every moment and in every person? Imagine the things that could happen.

After I walked away from the store that day, I knew the Lord had touched this man's heart and was already at work. He had been working on it before I got there, and I'd just been sent to plant seeds. We're all called to share our stories and to say, "I was lost, and I've been found." That's the good news! And many times, when we minister to others, they usually end up ministering to us.

What he asked me that day has profoundly impacted my life. I spent the rest of that trip contemplating what he had said. *Who am I? What is my calling?* Then I started to write down all the words that came to my mind: wounded healer, evangelist, speaker, singer, actress, child of light, and witness.

We all have a story, and we're all called to be a witness of God's mercy. In the Bible, when Jesus meets the woman at the well, He goes there at an unheard-of time of day—at noon. It must have been so hot and uncomfortable. Yet she's there because she probably feels like an outcast. She knows she's living a life of lies and unhappiness and doesn't know how to satisfy her thirst for love. Jesus goes into the unheard-of places, at the unheard-of times, and offers us His living water.

The woman was surprised that He spoke to her and asked her for a drink. He said, "If you knew the gift of God and who is saying to you, 'Give me a drink,' you would have asked Him, and He would have given you living water" (John 4:10).

The water He offers is a gift. It's free, and it's for all of us. It's the only water that will satisfy the deep thirst in our hearts. And at first, the woman was confused. She thought, *How could He possibly get water out of the well without a bucket?* But then she is given the light of understanding when He says, "Everyone who drinks of this water will be thirsty again, but whoever drinks the water I shall give will never thirst; the water I shall give will become in him a spring of water welling up to eternal life." When she hears that, she asks for the living water. Her greatest desires are true love and eternal life. Her most extraordinary thirst is not in her body but in her heart.

Jesus says, "Go call your husband and come back," and she says, "I do not have a husband." He replies, "You are right in saying 'I do not have a husband' for you have had five husbands, and the one you have now is not your husband. What you have said is true" (John 4:13–18).

When He said this, He didn't condemn her. He knew what was going on in her life and was bringing darkness to light with tenderness, mercy, and compassion. I can imagine that conversation—how Jesus looked into her eyes, and how it felt for someone to honestly know her, to know her calling, and to see something so good in her. His glance reminded her of who she was and what was truly important in life.

She put her water jar down and cast aside the things of her past. She rejected the false wells filled with counterfeit water that were dehydrating her and ruining her life. She came into a new life and her new identity.

Then, filled with God's living water, she became the first evangelist in the Bible and went running into the town to tell everyone the good news. She became a witness of God's mercy because she received unconditional and non-condemning love from our Savior—who redeems everything.

But she didn't stop there, and she didn't just share her story. She led others to Him, and then they encountered Him for themselves and believed. She found her calling—a witness of mercy and wounded healer with a vocation to love. Our vocation is to love everyone, to see Christ in everyone, and to bring people to Him.

 PICKING UP THE PIECES

I ask you: Who are you? What is your calling? What is God calling you to do today? How can you become a witness to His mercy? How can you live out the vocation to love? Who can you share His love with today? What encounters and circumstances have happened to you that can help you understand your life's purpose better?

Begin now to take time to think about who you truly are. (There's an appendix at the back of this book with some words to help you get started.)

PRAYER

Spend five minutes in silence every day this week, asking the Lord, "Who am I? What is my calling?" and see what He says.

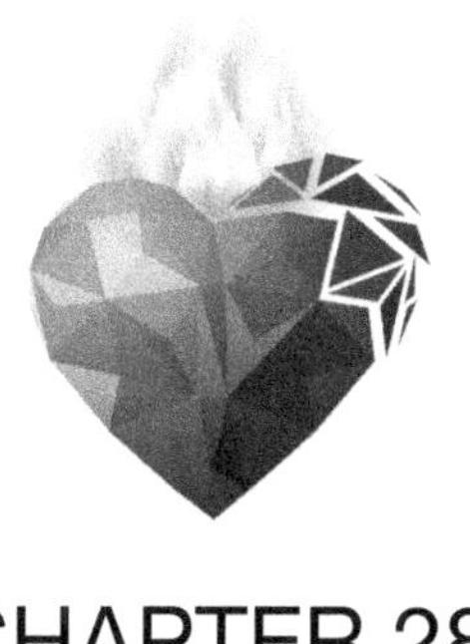

CHAPTER 28

FREEDOM IN CHRIST

The spirit of the Lord GOD is upon me, because the LORD has
anointed me; He has sent me to bring good news to the afflicted,
to bind up the brokenhearted, to proclaim liberty to the captives,
release to the prisoners.
—Isaiah 61:1

I continued to contemplate and pray about what the Lord was calling me to do and pondered the two phrases—*Who am I?* and *What is my calling?* Then more people began reaching out and asking me to speak at various places.

God always provides and always shows up, but the enemy often makes us doubt our giftings. So many times, I worried I wasn't a good enough speaker, and fear would overtake me on the day of an event, up to the very second of walking onto the stage or altar. Then the Holy Spirit took over, and instead, I was filled with deep peace.

When I first started speaking, I carried many papers with a ton of notes on them and was so afraid to let go. But I would hear the small and gentle whisper of the Holy Spirit, like a thought in the heart, asking me to put my papers down. Yet I was scared and believed the lie that I had a terrible memory and wouldn't know what to say.

Those insecurities persisted until one day, I was in a big auditorium preparing to give a talk to a large crowd. The person running the event had just introduced me, and as I was coming on stage, the announcer accidentally bumped into me. My notes flew all over—far too many to pick up.

With spotlights shining on my face, I tried to act calm and collected in front of the hundreds of people waiting for me to speak. The audience looked at me with eyes wide open wondering what was going to happen next. As I stared at them like a deer in headlights, I had no choice but to finally overcome my fears. I let the Holy Spirit take over, and ironically, it turned out to be one of the best talks I had ever given up to that point. It's as if the training wheels had come off whether I was ready or not. And when I prepare for talks now, I spend most of my time in prayer, develop an outline, and try to speak from my heart. It took a lot of surrender, but I finally learned to put my trust in God.

Also, before events, I often found myself repeatedly asking the Holy Spirit to show up, as if one time wasn't enough or He wasn't already present. Every day is a battle of letting go, but God is always there for us, and we need to remember He lives in us.

Others didn't see my anxiety and all of the lies that were still lodged in my heart. I continued to struggle at times with feelings of unworthiness because of the many years I spent away from God and the wounds that I had endured. But now, He was using me to help lead others to Him, and the passion inside had been ignited. I'd been given a new chance to love and wanted to fill my good column, so I did my part and showed up. By His grace, when I would get up to speak, the words just flowed out of my mouth, and I felt exhilarated.

The film *The Little Mermaid*[9] comes to mind. Ariel's special gift that brought joy and healing to others was her voice, and the enemy, "Ursula," wanted to take it away. In reality, our spiritual enemy wants to try to take away our voice. Imagine what the world would be like if we all spoke truth, built each other up, and sang divine praises each day.

Then after reading a book about Saint Ignatius of Loyola's Rules of Discernment, I began to better understand the lies of the enemy and see God's will more clearly. I was already praying for the healing of others, but I realized God wasn't done with my healing yet either. Honestly, until the day we die, He continues to heal us and bring us into new life. The lies don't ever stop coming, but now I can recognize them, reject them, and live freely.

In ministry, I've also come to notice how uncreative the enemy is. Most of us are struggling with the same things, and to see people living in new freedom brings so much delight to my heart.

If I had let my fear hold me back and hadn't kept moving forward, I would never have been able to bring the message of God's healing love to others. But as I pushed past fear, more speaking events and ministry opportunities opened up. I then had another encounter with the Lord that took years to understand and is still unraveling. However, it involved being His mouthpiece, and I knew I was being called to leave the youth ministry to venture out more into the speaking world. It was again a long discernment with the help of an excellent priest, who was my spiritual director.

During this transition, I also reached out for encouragement to a couple of speakers that were referred to me. I thought they would be excited and want to help, but two of them were very discouraging and told me how they had failed their first year and how difficult it was. While I believe they meant well and were just sharing what had happened to them, I was disturbed by their responses and didn't feel supported. It shook me up a bit as I was confused by their negativity and began to doubt again if I was on the right path. However, after a few tears, I brought it back to prayer, and God gave me clarity that He was calling me in this way. So I boldly took another leap of faith, and He provided.

I made many sacrifices, and the change certainly wasn't easy or glamorous by worldly standards. At the time, I only had a couple of speaking events lined up but was trusting God. And while I had many real-estate assets, I was unable to sell them for different reasons. Also, I didn't have much cash in the bank as I had already walked away from so much in order to do ministry.

My only option was to sell nearly all that I had left in material possessions—including my jewelry—so I did. While I felt afraid on the surface, a deep peace and feeling of strength reassured my heart that I was doing the right thing. I started with only four months' worth of expenses in my savings account and figured I would see what happened. I knew the results were in God's hands, and I humbled myself to give it my all so I would have no regrets. I only wanted to do His will and bring Him glory. Material things didn't hold a place in my heart anymore the way that they used to, and I felt free. I thought, *If this is how God wants to use me and provide for us, then so be it, but I won't know unless I try.*

At several points, my bank account dropped down to around $100, and I would cry out to the Lord. Often, He would quickly and miraculously provide a deposit through a new talk or a generous gift from someone who believed in the mission and was moved by the Holy Spirit to help.

I relied on God for everything and cried many tears that I wish I could get back. Things were often last minute, but God was never late! I wish I had trusted more in these moments, but my faith was built up over time, as I learned that God always keeps His promises.

But seek first the kingdom (of God) and his righteousness, and all of these things will be given you besides. Do not worry about tomorrow; tomorrow will take care of itself."
—Matthew 6:33-34

There is a big difference between doing something risky on our own just because we want to and doing something for God because He's asking it of us. God will never fail us. Although there definitely were ups and downs, my heart had never been more full of peace and contentment because I got to serve others.

I learned to live on very little and even chose to do without a personal credit card for many years so I could stay debt-free and rely solely on Divine Providence. I wanted to glorify the Lord with my life and only lived on what He provided. When we are being faithful witnesses and following God's will, He will keep our jars and hearts full.

"For the LORD, the God of Israel, says: 'The jar of flour shall not go empty, nor the jug of oil run dry, until the day when the LORD sends rain upon the earth.' She left and did as Elijah had said. She had enough to eat for a long time—he and she and her household. The jar of flour did not go empty, nor the jug of oil run dry, according to the word of the LORD spoken through Elijah."
—*1 Kings 17:14–16*

The Lord continued to bless me over time and keep my flour jar full in many ways, and for that I'm forever grateful. He also continued to affirm my calling.

Toward the beginning of the ministry while in Adoration, I asked the Lord if I was on the right path. At that moment, I received an invitation to speak at a small event. Only six people showed up, and I was confused about how this was an affirmation from God. But since He is a God of multiplication, that event miraculously led to eight more engagements over time, where I witnessed to several thousands of people. As we learn in the Bible, God can take five loaves and two fish and feed the multitudes. He's all about working with what we have, and the results and multiplication are in His hands.

Now, I'm not saying we are all to quit our jobs and pursue our dreams on our own. However, through deep prayer and spiritual guidance from authorities in our lives, we can trust in God to fulfill His promises. This is not a quick process to be rushed, and it takes discernment as everyone's calling will be different. But regardless of what you do, it can be considered ministry as you become the light of Christ to everyone around you.

As things continued to unfold, I regularly went to Adoration, asking God to "open the doors that need to be opened and close the doors that need to be closed." I knew this was His work, and I had no idea how to begin. However, I chose to make Jesus my CEO and made a list of saints to be on my board of directors. I spent countless hours asking the Lord for the next steps. Some days I got quick replies, and other days I became anxious again, but I persevered and He started to send people into my life to help with the ministry.

On one occasion, not being able to see much ahead, I began to get nervous again. However, the nerves subsided as I leaned on the Scriptures, made acts of faith, and chose to thank God ahead of time for what He was going to do.

"Have no anxiety at all, but in everything, by prayer and petition, with thanksgiving make your requests known to God."
—Philippians 4:6

In my prayer I said, "Lord, I don't want to doubt you anymore. I know this is your work and I'm just your servant. You have called me in this way, and you know where I'm supposed to go next and who you want me to meet. I've cried so many tears and don't want to dishonor you anymore. So I'm going to do the holiest thing I know how to do today and trust in you to take care of the rest. I'm excited to meet all of the people you will put in my path and ask that you touch and heal their hearts through me. Please bless us.

Thank you and now I'm going back to the holiest thing I can do today; I'm going to vacuum my house. I love you."

Sometimes household chores can be our greatest prayer if done for the love of God and others. As Saint Teresa of Avila said, "God walks among the pots and pans."

When I was done vacuuming, I saw that I had missed a call from a priest I know. I called him back and he said, "I was driving in my car, and you just came to my mind. I know we spoke a few months ago about you coming to the parish to give a talk. I would really love that. But the more I think about it, I would rather you give two talks instead of one." He proceeded to tell me his desire for the parish and the needs of those that would be attending. I thanked God for this opportunity, and the events were beautiful and moving. I always receive so much more than I can ever give and came home transformed, carrying all the people I met in my heart.

On another occasion, I wasn't going to attend a big event for my ministry because of the cost, but in prayer, I was nudged to go regardless of whether I had the funds. I ended up finding a plane ticket for a very low price and booked my flight on a leap of faith. The next morning, I checked my mailbox and found that I had received a generous gift. It came with a note of encouragement to continue to trust in God and how He's called me, and this moved me to tears of gratitude. God's work was being done, and He was providing as He promised. When we are faithful in little things, He begins to give us more.

As I continued to move forward and follow His promptings, He also inspired me to make a video and post it online. I knew He wanted someone to see it, I just didn't know who. I put it on social media while in Adoration and shortly after got an email from a well-known Catholic evangelist. On the phone, I heard four very powerful words. The person said, "I believe in you." Second to "I love you," these are the four most impactful words anyone can ever say. As I hung up the phone, this acknowledgment echoed in my heart, and I felt as if our Heavenly Father was saying them to me Himself. God knew I was shaking in fear when I posted the video. However, courage isn't about not being afraid, it's all about doing it anyway! The word "courage" comes from the Latin word cor, meaning heart. It's a matter of the heart, not a feeling.

I wish I could get back all of the moments I wasted worrying because the result was still the same. God was and IS in control. Surrendering isn't easy, but it brings joy. Mother Angelica said: "You want to do something for the Lord . . . do it. Whatever you feel needs to be done, even though you're shaking in your boots, you're scared to death—take the first step forward. The grace comes with that one step, and you get the grace as you step. Being afraid is not a problem; it's doing nothing when you're afraid."

It's difficult to push past our fears, but if we don't, we won't get to participate in God's plan for us, and ultimately, that's where our happiness lies. We're constantly growing and learning, and as we grow, we learn to recognize our weaknesses and how God can set us free from them. We can begin to see patterns and notice things in other people's lives as well to help them.

I can't say enough about the importance of Holy Scripture and how the truth does set us free to be who we are called to be.

"For freedom Christ set us free; so stand firm and do not submit again to the yoke of slavery."
—*Galatians 5:1*

Once we are firmly rooted in our identity as beloved children of God, we begin to see everything in the light and can boldly rejoice in God's plans for us. I don't know why we have so much self-doubt. It's easy to say, "Why would God use me? Why would he give me anything? Look at my past. Look at where I came from," but the past is part of our story. What if Paul had stayed Saul—a murderer? What if Saint Mary Magdalene, from whom seven demons were cast out, stayed demonized? Or what if Saint Peter, who denied Jesus after knowing Him and encountering Him, stayed in that denial and didn't turn back? There would be no good news, but God does want to use us no matter what we've done, and no matter where we've been. We just need to surrender and place our trust in Him.

Each of us has a different set of gifts, and we're all destined to be saints of different causes. But to do the good work, we need to go out into the world and speak life into the hearts of others to help set captives free. We are all in ministry to those around us and just need to take the first step forward. God will propel us and sustain us in our missions.

The sacrifices He asks will no longer frighten us; instead, we will fear not doing them, as our greatest treasure will be found in heaven. Now, I'm not saying that earthly wealth is bad, but an attachment to it is. It should never become an idol and must always be viewed as belonging to God, who can give and take away. As Saint John of the Cross said in a spirit of great detachment, "Now that I no longer desire all, I have it all without desire."

 PICKING UP THE PIECES

Where are you attacked the most? What lies run through your mind that hold you back or make it difficult to use a gift to help others? How have you been dealing with doubts and fears? What Bible verses help you to overcome these falsehoods?

PRAYER

Lord Jesus, you are our healer. Please bring to light the lies that are holding us back from serving you more deeply. Please set us free, and may your truth be deeply rooted in our hearts. Help us to hear your small whisper telling us the truth of who we are and what we are capable of in you! Amen.

CHAPTER 29

RESTORED DREAMS

But the plan of the LORD stands forever,
the designs of his heart through all generations.
—Psalm 33:11

As I proceeded to say yes to God, He continued to bless me. More people began reaching out saying they felt the world needed to hear my message, and new opportunities began to open up.

I ended up on several international TV shows sharing the good news! And God's promise was being fulfilled as the message He gifted me with to help others miraculously reached millions around the world.

> *"But you will receive power when the holy Spirit comes upon you, and you will be my witnesses in Jerusalem, throughout Judea and Samaria, and to the ends of the earth."*
> —*Acts 1:8*

On one of the TV shows, in addition to the interview, we filmed a scene with me kneeling in an Adoration Chapel and praying. The shoot took several hours, but I could feel the love of God with us, and I kept thanking Him over and over again for this remarkable opportunity to film something for His glory.

When we were done with the shoot, the producer came up to me with a serious look on his face. He apologized for surrounding me with that many candles and for so long. I looked at him, stunned, as I realized I hadn't even been aware of the big, tall candles around me or experienced any fear the entire time. My fear of fire had been overcome by the fire inside of me.

My desire for others to know the love of God and to have a prayerful relationship with Him had overtaken me. Here I was, the girl who didn't know what an Adoration Chapel was when she returned to the church—now leading others in Adoration. Here I was, the girl who was afraid of fire, now surrounded by it yet unafraid. Saint Joan of Arc's words echoed within me: "I am not afraid . . . I was born to do this."

When we face our fears and move forward with God's will, we will eventually be able to step into the roles He intended for us all along. We just have to surrender and keep on going.

Then, shockingly, everything went into upheaval as a pandemic swept through the world, killing many people and causing so much devastation. My talks got canceled or went virtual, and I had no idea what I was going to do.

However, during this time of reflection, the Lord inspired me to produce a film based on my conversion story to continue reaching those in need. My film, *Fully Known*, which is about identity in Christ, was conceived in my heart and I felt as if I would burst if I held it in. I gave everything I had at the time to get it made and others who believed in the project gave generous contributions as well.

By the grace of God, it aired to hundreds of millions of people on a Catholic television network and competed with multimillion-dollar projects at some of the largest Christian film festivals in the world. The film was nominated for twenty-three awards total and won four. I won two "Best Actress" awards and found myself on the red carpet at film festivals glorifying God. All of this was certainly miraculous as these results were in His hands. I was finally using my gifts for Him, and it was so redeeming given my past especially, when I had left my dreams behind for so many years because someone told me I wouldn't and couldn't make it.

When we surrender to God, He levels the playing fields and resurrects our dreams and the truth of who we are in Him. He begins to place His dreams in our hearts—ones so much better than we could ever come up with on our own.

It had also been stirring within me to be a TV host again. It fit in with my speaking, and I had co-hosted a show in the past. On my grandma's birthday a few months after her death, my graphic designer sent me my new TV hosting résumé. Then, the phone rang about an hour later. An international TV network said my name came to them in prayer when discerning a new host for a show focused on faith-based film and television. I, of course, told them that this was in my prayer too and had just refreshed my résumé.

I never even had to send it to anyone and can only attribute this to God. He is the one with all the connections, and I thank my grandma for her intercession too. Whenever I tried to connect with someone on my own, it didn't work. But with anyone God sent to me, it's as if He showed them a glimpse of Himself and the mission within me. Though I did my best to work hard and follow any inspirations that I thought were from Him, I knew He was in charge of the outcome.

During the pandemic, I was able to record the show virtually from home until travel opened up again. This was certainly not an easy time, for me or many people around the world. Along with others, I suffered moments of great pain and sorrow. However, God did continue to bring beauty from the ashes.

On the TV show, I've had the opportunity to interview many celebrities and public figures, including people from my prior life in Hollywood. But now it's for God's purposes, and only He could see that our meeting back then would have such a beautiful and profound purpose in the future.

As the Lord continued to put my life back together, the pieces of my past began to make more sense. Through this new TV show, the Lord also redeemed the broken piece created by the hosting agent who had said years earlier that I was missing a "spark." Clearly, God has given me one since, and He has the final say. Surrendering to Divine Providence daily isn't easy, but it allows God to work miracles in our lives.

Then travel started to open back up. I was once again flying around the country and eventually the world to share about the healing power of God's love and our call to fill our good columns. Healing and evangelism through speaking, prayer, and the arts are my mission.

At one point, I was also inspired to go to The Shrine of Our Lady of Schoenstatt to pray and ask the Lord if He wanted me to do more acting. It had always been one of my deepest desires since I was a little girl, but I only wanted to do so if it was His will. I had such a peace in my heart when pondering it but still wanted His affirmation.

When I pulled into the parking lot of the shrine, I immediately received a text message about a new film focused on The Eucharist. They asked if I would be interested in being in it, and without hesitating, I said yes. I didn't know what role I would play and thought maybe I would get cast for a small part. However, I prayed and asked the Lord to inspire the director to put me in the role that He wanted me in. Little did I know that He would choose me to play the Blessed Mother. Being in OCDS had already prepared me to study her life and heart, and now I was being called to go even deeper in my love and understanding of her.

I will never portray a greater person in my lifetime, and it was a dream I had never even dared to dream but was hidden deep inside of me. Only God could give me the strength and grace to play the Blessed Mother, but one thing is certain, He had my "yes!"

As I began my preparation for the role, at first it felt like a heavy burden as I wanted to be as perfect as her but realized that wasn't possible. Over time, though, I was able to accept that it was a true honor, and I was putting too much pressure on myself. I actually feel like I didn't "play" the role but rather "prayed" the role.

God doesn't ask us to be perfect. He just looks at the disposition of our hearts and our intents. Undoubtedly, I will spend the rest of my existence pondering her life and trying to be more like the Blessed Mother, a reflection of Christ. It's a role I will never be able to finish studying as the depths are beyond my comprehension.

When we turn to the Lord, He makes our dreams come true. We often find they were His dream all along, but we allowed fear or selfishness to get in the way. When we are living an authentic Christian life, we can and should expect God to direct our desires—we just need to let Him. Today, let us open our hearts and ask Him to place His dreams in them, so that we may bring Him glory. And for all the people in our lives who ever said, "You can't do that, you're not good enough, and you won't." God instead says, "You can do it, you are good enough, and you will accomplish it—in Me! I will open doors for you that no one can shut, and I will bless you with a mission."

"I know your works (behold, I have left an open door before
you, which no one can close)."
—Revelation 3:8

 PICKING UP THE PIECES

Are there any broken dreams that you need God to heal or restore?

Have you ever asked Him to place His dream for you in your heart?

How have you responded to inspirations in the past? What opportunities has the Lord put in your path that help reveal His will for you?

Do you realize that God is your defender and will help make your dreams come true?

PRAYER

Heavenly Father, your dream for our lives is so much bigger and better than anything we could ever think of on our own. Please place your dream for us in our hearts, and give us the grace and strength to follow through. Amen.

CHAPTER 30

FEELING OTHERS' PAIN

For the whole law is fulfilled in one statement, namely,
"You shall love your neighbor as yourself."
—Galatians 5:14

As the Lord began to place His dream in my heart, I also started to spend time noticing the poor and the suffering more. You may have heard the phrase, "What would Jesus do?" If we asked ourselves this question more often, I'm sure our response patterns in daily life would be so much different. We are all saints in the making. We just need to keep choosing to do the right thing.

In addition to the way the Lord called me to serve Him through speaking and the arts, I also knew it was important to be involved in community service. For several years, I went on a monthly truck run where we encountered the poor. We brought them food, water, clothing, and most importantly, love.

The first stop we made was under a highway overpass where a group of homeless individuals lived. Over the years, we grew close to them and knew one another by name. I thought of them as family and loved them very much. However, as time passed, some disappeared, often without us knowing where they went or if they were still alive. When that happened, it was like losing a loved one, and a time of grief followed. We had no choice but to entrust them to the Lord and believe that they were in His tender care.

The next place we went was a low-income motel, and to get there, we passed through an impoverished part of town. The motel itself was nearly falling apart, and the paint was chipping on the outside. In the air was a moldy smell mixed with body odor, and the windows were covered with sheets and towels. Many of the tenants had to share common areas with their neighbors as well, and we had seen our share of what looked like possible drug deals going on.

I can't imagine how unsafe it must have felt to sleep there at night, especially not knowing what was happening next door. We encountered many people with addictions as well and some in the greatest pits of despair and loneliness. Many struggled with hopelessness, meaninglessness, and extreme fear of the future.

Yet we also encountered those who looked out for their neighbor, and a deep feeling of community existed there. Sometimes someone asked for food and clothing for another person who wasn't home at the moment. Somehow, there always seemed to be light amid the darkness.

I have often seen fierce care and love among those who have next to nothing because there is very little in their way. They don't have all of the distractions in the world tempting and alluring them. In contrast, I ponder how I see emotional homelessness, extreme emptiness, and many violations against the commandment to "love your neighbor as yourself" in several affluent neighborhoods. It's easy to forget that we are created for community, and in our woundedness, sometimes that's hard to see. May God continue to bring darkness to light so that we can fulfill our calling to love.

Those who stayed at the motel were usually on and off the streets or very close to homelessness. One summer evening, it was around 104 degrees upon arrival, and when we got out of the truck, a man immediately caught my attention. He was probably in his sixties but looked much older. His face was drawn, he was sweating, appeared worn down, and hadn't shaved in a while. His hair was a mess, and his clothes were all stained. He looked beyond rugged, and as he walked very slowly toward us, it was as if he was in slow motion. It appeared that he was carrying the weight of the world on his shoulders.

As we prepared a massive bag of food and gave it to him, I felt prompted to ask about his story and how he had gotten there. He proceeded to tell us that he was very depressed, because he had worked for his best friend, who betrayed and fired him with no notice. There wasn't much in his checking account, nothing in savings, and all he could afford was that motel. He only had enough money for a few more days and was about to be homeless for the first time. Since he was suffering from so much sadness, he didn't even have the energy to look for a job. Overwhelmed and scared, he asked if we could pray for him.

I gladly led him in prayer to surrender his life to Jesus and repent of any sin. In the name of Jesus, he forgave his friend for the pain of his situation. Then we proceeded to pray together, asking Jesus to help heal him. And at the end of the prayer, he let out a thunderous wail, which was an alarming sound that lasted for nearly thirty seconds. I wasn't sure at first if it was a good thing or not, but what I saw afterward showed me that it was in fact positive—and he appeared healed.

I noticed three signs of healing. The first one was that this man's entire face lit up. The man who had seemed dead before was now alive! The second sign was that he couldn't stop saying, "Thank you, Jesus, thank you, Jesus, thank you, Jesus." He was praising the Lord, and I could tell his hope was restored. But the third sign of healing really blew my mind. As he shook the giant bag of food we gave him, he said with extreme excitement, "Now I can finally eat, now I can finally eat!"

That astonished me and touched my heart. Here we were giving a bag of food to a man who was supposed to be hungry and had no money for food. But if we had just handed it to him and walked away, he wouldn't have even been able to eat it.

He told us he had been so down that he hadn't had an appetite and had been unable to eat for days. We realized his heart was hungry and was the first thing that needed to be fed. And from this healing, his body was restored, and he could finally function again.

This experience made me wonder what might have happened if we hadn't gone one step further and given him the love and attention he needed? Would we be in community with one another? Are we taking the time to nourish and feed each other's hearts? Are we even aware of the hunger in our own?

We are all called to feed hungry hearts and become the face of God to others. It's love alone that heals and restores, and to give love is to give life. We can breathe life into another by taking time to notice them, listen to them, and pray with them.

 PICKING UP THE PIECES

Read this quote once with your head and then a second and third time slowly with your heart and ponder these questions:

How can you help feed someone else's hungry heart today? How can you become God's hands and feet in this lonely world?

"Christ has no body but yours, no hands, no feet on earth but yours, yours are the eyes with which he looks with compassion on this world.

Yours are the feet with which he walks to do good.

Yours are the hands with which he blesses all the world."

—St. Teresa of Avila

PRAYER

Lord Jesus, help us to be your hands and feet in this world and become your face to others. May we see everyone with your compassion and tender heart and may we all be restored in your name. Please feed and heal our hungry hearts. Amen.

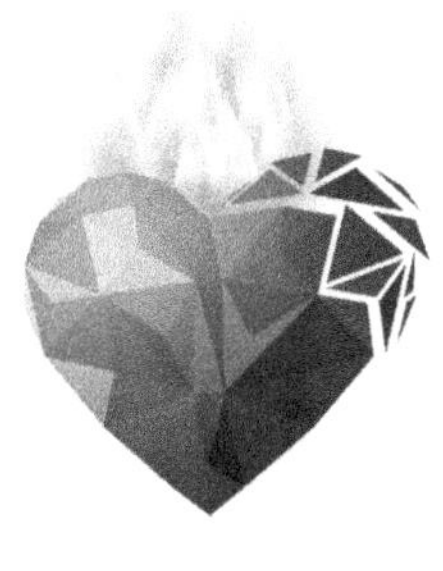

HOPE AND RESURRECTION

*Jesus told her, "I am the resurrection and the life; whoever
believes in me, even if he dies, will live."*
—John 11:25

To see the homeless man restored to life was beautiful and
redemptive. My grandma (Anna, who went by Anne) was
Italian and certainly had a gift for cooking and feeding hungry
hearts! Growing up, I remember her dishes with big yellow flowers
on the bottom of them. She would pile the food sky-high and say
to me, "Joelle, make sure you eat until you can see the flowers." It
was so delicious that there was never a problem finishing!

She fed me breakfast, lunch, and many times dinner, but
most importantly, she also fed my heart. She knew that I didn't
have an easy childhood, and that there was much suffering in my

home. However, she looked past all my woundedness and saw the good in me.

She always told me she believed in me and to trust in God. That seemed to be her answer to everything. It was profoundly simple, but it was the foundation for a life of miracles. My grandma was a living miracle herself and never forgot where she came from. Whether it was prayer, a financial gift, or the best bowl of pasta, she gave generously to all in need. And as a godmother to over thirty migrant children and a devout prayer warrior, her phone would ring off the hook with requests day and night.

At age ninety-four, my grandmother received a call for help from her ninety-six-year-old sister Millie, who was returning from the hospital. She wasn't well enough to stay home alone, and Grandma didn't hesitate to invite her to stay at her house as she wanted to cook and care for her.

The pandemic had just started, and there was much panic and uncertainty in the air, as little was known about this disease. It was spreading rapidly, and I was very concerned. I told Grandma it wasn't safe for her to take care of Aunt Millie, especially with the symptoms she was experiencing. However, she replied she wanted her there, and they were having a great time together. I can still hear them giggling and being silly like little girls. They even made prank calls to other family members just for fun.

Sadly, Aunt Millie did have the illness and ended up in the hospital. Shortly after, my fears were confirmed—Grandma got it and ended up there as well.

I trembled at the thought of her being alone and wanted to be there with her so badly, but she was quarantined, and they weren't allowing any visitors. I felt as if my heart was being stretched apart as it wanted to be in two places at once but couldn't. And my entire family was suffering, as they wouldn't let any of us in to see her. Unfortunately, everything progressed quickly, and the doctors informed us that she wouldn't make it.

My life was turned upside down once again as the woman who had saved my life with her prayers would die in the hospital alone. She was always there for me, and I couldn't be there for her in this hour of need—my heart was torn.

We were so close that my own mother had nicknamed me "Annie Jr." Grandma was my best friend, and we spoke almost every day of my entire life. I had only one main prayer request from her all these years, and it was for a "happy death." That was all that she asked for. I think she intuitively knew that she would suffer as she had a strong devotion to the passion of Jesus. God knows I faithfully prayed this intention for her many times over the years, and I envisioned her dying during Holy Communion, peacefully in her sleep or surrounded by loved ones. Never did I imagine her being alone.

This situation devastated my entire family as we were all so close to her. Many other family members were also sick, some with severe symptoms, some with none. First, our beloved Aunt Millie passed away in the hospital, and now my grandmother—our matriarch—was dying. It was the worst tragedy in our lives since the fire.

The enemy didn't waste any time trying to attack me with lies. I could barely breathe and was gasping for air as he assailed me with thoughts like, *If God loves you, why would he take away another one of the closest people from you? Why would He let her die such a cruel death? He wants to leave you all alone. You have no one left to love you. God is annihilating and taking away your entire family.* I was crying and grieving in pain, curled up in a ball on my shower floor. It was a familiar place that brought up the memory of my sister dying and feeling lost during my years away from the church. The main difference is that I realized what was happening this time and decided to stop believing the lies.

I once again turned to God in prayer, but thankfully I didn't pull away from Him like I did when I was little. Now I turned toward Him and leaned into Him for an answer. I wasn't afraid to ask Him questions and wasn't scared anymore to hear His response, which would be revealed over the next few critical days.

When we turn toward Christ and not away during the trials in our lives, we begin to live in truth. I think of Jesus when Lazarus died. He wept. Not only because of His own pain but also because of the pain He saw the others around Him experiencing. He was deeply troubled in spirit, and in His merciful compassion, He brought Lazarus back to life through the love of Our Father—for His glory.

Is there something you're going through right now that you desperately need the Lord to bring back to life? What are you grieving over that is causing affliction? A broken relationship? A broken dream? The loss of a loved one? The loss of a job? Abandonment? Loneliness? Whatever it is, realize that Jesus is grieving with you. His heart is stirred with love, and He's longing to bring you resurrection in that area.

We need to remember that the enemy will tell us lies that go against the resurrection in our lives. He does this because he's terrified of what the world would look like if we all lived with a resurrection mentality. Suppose we knew that none of our problems were too big for God. That despite our heartaches, there's still a purpose for our lives, and that we don't die but live forever in heaven.

The enemy wants to paint a picture of a mean God who wants to take everything away from us and doesn't care, but the truth is that the love of God is so great and unfathomable. He longs to redeem our hurts and restore us to life. And while our grief isn't going away, trusting in God makes it bearable.

During Grandma's last few days in the hospital, the nurses were so kind. One of them even allowed us to do a video call with her a few times. Many family members were on the call, and we told her how much we loved her and that we were with her in our hearts. Although she couldn't move, her eyes opened, and I knew she was aware that it was us.

Nearly every day of my life, she would joke around with me and say in Italian that one day I would call and she would not answer. She thought it was funny at the time and I would ask her to stop saying that and stop talking about her death.

Although she lived many years, I realized that those words had just become prophetic. I was calling her on the phone and she couldn't answer. It's as if she secretly always knew her death would be this way, even if she didn't know exactly how it would happen.

Her face resembled the crucified Jesus, and it didn't even seem like I was looking at my grandma anymore but rather Jesus Himself. He's all I could see as she was transformed and became one with Christ through her suffering. I also don't think it's a coincidence that she was in the hospital during Holy Week, and shortly after Easter would be her resurrection.

On the last day of her life, a new nurse was on duty, and when I called, she said, "I just got done saying the Hail Mary prayer for your grandma." I was amazed and asked her how she had known to do that. I had told several of the other nurses it was her favorite prayer and asked them to say it with her, so I thought maybe they had put it in her chart. The nurse replied, "There's a big whiteboard in her room that says for everyone that enters to say a Hail Mary for Anne." It was even printed out for those who didn't know the prayer. What a beautiful act of love and comfort amid a fiery trial. My grandma was evangelizing even on her deathbed!

Later that day, the nurse held the phone to my grandmother's ear for almost two hours. I prayed the Rosary and Divine Mercy Chaplet and told her everyone loved her, naming all of our family members. Then, taking a moment of silence, I asked God to give me the right words as I realized the gravity of the moment. I didn't know what to say to the most incredible woman in the world—the woman who saved me, fed me, and led me. Then the following words bubbled up and came out of my mouth in strength mingled with tears: "Grandma, nothing can ever separate us. We are all together forever. Love never dies." When I said this, the nurse got back on the phone and told me she had passed.

I was in awe. While tears were streaming down my face, I found myself praising God for His omniscience. Only He could measure a life down to the last words and last breath to prove that LOVE NEVER DIES.

These precious words made way for hope and affirmation that He raised her. I believe she passed to heaven and to new life, and I'm sure that she offered all of her suffering up to save many souls.

When we unite our suffering with Christ, it becomes redemptive. Nothing here on earth done with love is ever wasted. We will only understand it all once we get to heaven.

Saint Mother Teresa said, "I have found the paradox, that if you love until it hurts, there can be no more hurt, only more love." Similarly, Saint John Paul II once said, "It is suffering more than anything else, which clears the way for grace which transforms human souls. Suffering more than anything else, makes present in the history of humanity, the powers of redemption."

My grandma's happy death wasn't what I had envisioned, but it was happy indeed. She suffered during Lent with Jesus. She got to hear her granddaughter, who was once so lost but saved by her prayers, praying for her. While she always prayed for others, in the end, she got to see the fruits of her labors.

I'm sure she was surrounded by all of heaven and reunited with Poppy, Maria, her siblings, and her parents, whom she lost at such a young age. Grandma passed just a day after Divine Mercy Sunday and during the Easter season. She indeed rose with Christ.

I sometimes think about the Blessed Mother at the foot of the cross. There is no question that she cried as she witnessed her son's brutal crucifixion. Although she knew His sacrificial love would save humanity, she was one with Him and loved Him deeply. The pain of seeing Jesus suffering pierced her own heart as she suffered with Him. Even after the Ascension and knowing He was in Heaven, I can imagine that she missed making a meal for Him and hugging Him.

Grief is part of our lives here, part of loving and being human. The deeper we love, the deeper we grieve. It's not that we won't suffer in this life, but rather that our eyes need to be focused on heaven. How we react to the grief in our lives and how deeply we are connected with the heart and cross of Jesus will make the difference. Do we see Him raise our loved ones and issues in life with our spiritual eyes, or do we lose hope and think that all is left in the tomb and hopeless? Today Jesus is asking us to hear His voice calling our name. He wants us to break free from the lies that entomb us and remember, as Saint John Paul II said, "We are the Easter people and Alleluia is our song."

When my sister died in the house fire, I couldn't see things with eyes of faith. I didn't see her resurrection and thought God didn't love me or hear my prayer. But through this experience with my grandma, God redeemed that memory. Now I can see that He did raise my sister—it just didn't look how I expected.

I have a picture of Grandma and me from a while ago, and her eyes are looking up. We took several photos that day and in none of them was she looking at the camera because she always had her eyes on heaven.

And through her relationship with God and the trials in her life, she became understanding and compassionate toward all the people she encountered. She became the hands and feet of Christ in the world and died trying to save another.

This amazing woman lit up a room when she walked in, and everyone wanted whatever she had. Her secret strength and glow came from her prayer life, and she left a trail of light everywhere she went. She set the world on fire and left a legacy of Love, which is our calling too.

"Be who God created you to be, and you will
set the world on fire."
—St. Catherine of Siena

 PICKING UP THE PIECES

Have you ever prayed for something that came true but didn't look like what you thought it would? Have you ever lost someone you were very close to and questioned God why they had to die or leave the way they did? How are you handling the trials and fires in your life? Are you turning away from God or toward Him? What are some good memories you have of those that have passed? What can you learn from their lives?

PRAYER

Heavenly Father, you have our lives planned down to the last breath. When tragedy strikes, it's difficult for us to see your loving hand. Please help us to know that you are with us and love us. I know when we get to heaven, it will all make sense. Please help us with our grief and heal us in your merciful heart. Amen.

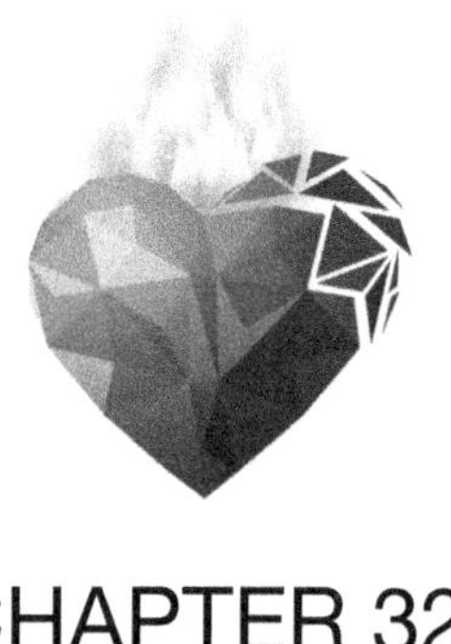

CHAPTER 32

MOVING FORWARD

I have come to set the earth on fire,
and how I wish it were already blazing!
—Luke 12:49

My grandma was so alive in Christ that she set the world on fire and left a trail ablaze with her love. Even after her death, it's only growing. How can we leave a legacy of love when we pass? Where and when are the opportunities to do so?

Once the Lord begins to heal our lives, He calls us to heal others. With our eyes are open, we will start to see the opportunities to help others and be more present. God is the great "I AM." He is not stuck in the past or the future as He is outside of space and time. He is with us always and is constantly trying to communicate with us, and He wants to use us to bring His love into the world.

The person right in front of us is our calling at the moment, and since we are judged on love, we need to evaluate how well we love. And I'm not just talking about the people that love us back, but what about those who feel forgotten about and with no one to love them? What about our enemies? How can we love the people who have hurt us?

It takes a hero's heart to forgive and love without expecting anything in return. But it's true that the more we give, the more we receive. As Saint John of the Cross said, "Put love, where there is no love, and find love." Even if we don't feel love returned from the person we give it to, we will find God's sacrificial love inside of us. It's a supernatural, superhero kind of love that can only be accomplished through Love Himself.

When my son, Blake, was little, he loved superheroes. Honestly, I don't think any of us ever outgrow them. And while God didn't miraculously use His superpowers to raise my sister from the dead when I was little, I now have seen Him raise countless others from spiritual death to life. My children have witnessed this too when the Lord has put people in our path, at the beach or even in ordinary places like a home-improvement store. They have seen the power of prayer, taking time to notice others and love them when they are in need. There have been unexplainable moments when our hearts are being touched so deeply that we can't deny that God is with us. His love is without bounds, and He's constantly seeking us out, wanting to heal our hearts and empower us to live in His will. This is what happens as we strive for daily conversion to know, love, and serve Him.

One day, Blake asked me, "Mamma, are you Wonder Woman? You kind of look like her." I thought that was so funny and laughed. He was wearing his Spiderman T-shirt, which said, "I'm not saying I'm Spiderman; I'm just saying you haven't seen me and Spiderman in the same place before." So I said to him, "You know what your T-shirt says about Spiderman? Well, I'm not saying I'm Wonder Woman. I'm just saying you haven't seen me and Wonder Woman in the same place before." He giggled, then looked at me and said, "Mamma, I'm serious. Are you Wonder Woman?" And I said, "Honey, if I was, you know I couldn't tell you anyway."

I thought it was hysterical and left it at that, but he wouldn't let it go. A couple of weeks later, he said again, "You kind of look like her. Are you Wonder Woman?" And I finally said, "Honey, I'm not Wonder Woman like you're thinking, but we're all called to be superheroes for God." He said, "See? Was it that hard? You could have just told me that the first time." About ten minutes later, and with a look of suspicion on his face, he said, "You know, Mamma, you kind of hesitated before you answered me. Are you sure you're not Wonder Woman? I think you're hiding something."

Again, I laughed, and even now I joke around about it with him, because by the grace of God, I did end up in a film playing the role of the real Wonder Woman—the Blessed Mother. Only God saw that one coming! But the truth is, we are all called to be superheroes for God.

We're all called to be fully alive in the giftings that He's given us and in a deep, intimate relationship with Him. It's a place where our lives become supernatural and infused with divine grace. We realize we have no power but God's power, which is made perfect in weakness.

We have a God who can and does perform miracles, and in our weakness, we're made strong in Him. Clothed in humility, knowing who we are, where we came from, what we're created for, and seeing God work in us is what makes us superheroes in Christ—in His power for His glory. That's when we begin to walk not with human confidence but God confidence.

I think of Saint Joan of Arc who was being burned alive for her faithfulness to the Lord. Strengthened in the moment and filled with the power of God, she kept her eyes and heart on Jesus. She had a priest stand in front of her with a crucifix as she triumphantly asked him to hold the cross higher so she could see it through the flames! May we say these words with her during the fiery trials in our lives.

We're called to set the world on fire. We're called to be courageous, not to live in fear. We're called to live transparently. Saint Augustine said, "This is the very perfection of man, to find out his own imperfections." The more that comes to the surface, the more we understand our true identity. We can then begin to face outward and become bread for others in order to feed hungry hearts. We can do nothing without God, but we can do all things in Him.

For years after the house fire and losing my sister, I feared fire. I feared candles. I feared flames. If I smelled smoke of any kind, it brought back memories of the worst and most tragic night of my whole life. The smell of fire was so frightening and left me in a cloud of blackness and despair. However, through encountering Christ and experiencing the power of His love, I began to know that I was created for a purpose. A fire nearly took my life, but another fire saved it. A new fire started to live in me, and I was able to push past the things I used to fear—the things that were keeping me from my purpose and happiness in life.

To this day, the fire within continues to grow. When the fire of love is raging inside, I want to let the world know of God's love and goodness. We are called to become the fire. We are called to become a beacon of light, the Children of Light who bring radiance to the darkness of this world. We're called to be set free in the love of God, not to live in fear and not to be consumed by the flames.

"When you walk through fire, you shall not be burned,
nor will flames consume you."
—Isaiah 43:2

We need to keep our eyes on the Lord as we experience the flames of life. Through all the trials, tribulations, distractions, and hurts, we must trust that He is there. We will not be burned. We need to keep our true identity and stay rooted in Him. It's when we take our eyes off Him and start to look at all the fires raging around us and say, "Lord, did you see this? Did you see that?" Then we stop trusting and begin to lose our way.

We can't fear the fire. The fires are not going away. New ones are sprouting up all the time, but we need to keep our eyes on Christ. I think of the movie *Rocky*,[10] where Rocky says, "It's not about how hard you can hit, it's about how hard you can get hit and keep moving forward." We're going to get hit. We're going to get burned in some way at some time, but that doesn't mean that it will stop us. It doesn't mean it has to hurt in the same way it did in the past. We can keep moving forward, offer up our suffering and persevere, knowing who we are in Christ. We can live in our true identity as children of God.

My heart shattered into the tiniest pieces imaginable when my sister died. The thought of ever being whole again didn't even seem possible. I thought my life was over as the flames of discouragement, grief, and purposelessness enveloped me. I allowed the culture, the world, sin, and other people to take away my identity through the years.

My heart's pieces, broken into all different shapes and sizes, became more fragmented over time. On my own, I could never figure out how to put them back together, but God can do the impossible. He can take our most horrendous situations, mistakes, failures, and grievances and bring good out of them. If He had raised my sister from the dead on the day that I asked Him to, I don't believe I would be doing what I am today and with the passion that sustains me. The Lord has redeemed the most tragic circumstances of my life to bring hope and healing to others.

By His grace, I have now witnessed countless people being brought from death to life by experiencing the love and truth of God. I have seen people's faces lift and light up, and their bodies become animated when they finally discover that God loves them and has a plan for their lives.

We may feel broken and unrepairable, but there is no Gospel without redemption—Jesus died to save us and can heal our deepest wounds. He brings beauty from the ashes and nothing is outside of His providence. Nothing can overcome the good He can accomplish through us.

We are never too far gone, too bruised, or too wounded for God to put back together. We become fully alive, more vibrant, and more beautiful than we could have ever imagined—in Him. He has a plan and is not done with us yet. And we can make a difference in the world, especially when we come together and love as He's called us to.

Let us rise, pick up our mats, and walk. Let us move forward, trusting in His promise to restore, redeem, and empower us. He—and only He—defines us.

He and only He is the Master of our pieces.

♡ PICKING UP THE PIECES

We need to focus on our good column. If we focus on who we are and what we are created for and love one another, then we're not sinning. Our identity is in Christ, and we are who He says we are. The Bible tells us so. Above all, let us read and tell His story, and may our story become HIStory! Surrender to a daily relationship with Him. There is no other way to happiness. Be in conversation and communion with the Lord. Meditate on the Scriptures and let His Word sink into your heart. God's love NEVER fails, and God's love NEVER dies.

PRAYER

Lord Jesus, thank you for being the Master of my pieces. Thank you for the healing I've experienced already. I ask that you continue to heal my life. May I never forget who I am in you. Please continue to help me through the various trials and fires in life so that I don't get burned. May the fire of your love grow fervently in my heart. Thank you for dying to save me and for the plans you have for my future. Jesus, I trust in you. Amen.

APPENDIX

WHO AM I?

Beloved
Protected
Prayer warrior
Soldier for Christ
Provided for
Beautiful
Prophet
Wounded Healer
Made new
Adopted
Good friend
Faith-filled
Peaceful
Inspiring
Knowledgeable
Confident
Sweet
Blessed
Honored
Loveable
Caring
Compassionate
Not alone
A good sister
Intuitive
Kind
Loving
Sensitive
A child of God
Daughter
Child of light
Chosen
Favored
Trusted
Raised
Saved
Delivered
Graced

Redeemed
Healed
Free
Part of a community
A believer
Christian
Survivor
Found
Strengthened
Hopeful
Strong
A gift
A treasure
Holy
Pure
Forgiven
Giving
Peacemaker
Merciful
Disciple
Joyful
Brave
Spiritual mother
Leader
Smart
Bold
Open
Seeking Christ
Witness
Unique
Blossoming
Focused
Delightful
Virtuous
Loving
Peacemaker
Adventurous
Trusting

Worthy
Encouraging
Evangelist
Cherished
Gracious
Called
Special
Trusting
Made in His image
A reflection
Sacred
Sound-minded
Strong
One of a Kind
Accepted
Royalty
Clean
Sanctified
New
Enough
Fully Known
Renewed
Hopeful
A Delight
Adopted
Seen
Victorious
Gifted
Talented
Alive
Spirit-filled
Planned
His
Masterpiece
Restored
Redeemed
Empowered
Perfectly Loved

PUTTING THE PIECES OF YOUR STORY TOGETHER

What was your relationship like with God as a child?

____

____

____

____

As a teen?

____

____

____

____

As an adult?

____

____

____

____

Name three main broken pieces in your life.

____

____

____

____

Name a time God tried to shine light through your broken piece (for example, through circumstance, a Scripture, or another way).

____

____

____

____

Was there a turning point where you surrendered your life to the Lord? If so, what happened?

____

____

____

____

What did you change in your life after that?

____

____

____

____

If there has not been a turning point yet, what broken pieces has the Lord been bringing to mind? What steps can you make to allow Him to heal you so you can encounter His love more deeply—prayer, going to church, joining a Bible study, etc.?

____

____

____

____

What are your unique gifts and talents?

____

____

____

____

How may the Lord be calling you to help others?

____

____

____

____

Be ready to share your story with someone in need. You never know who you can help. God is with us!

NOTES

1) Saint John Paul II, *Catechism of the Catholic Church*, 2nd ed., (Washington, DC: United States Catholic Conference, 2011), sec. 782, accessed at https://www.usccb.org/sites/default/files/flipbooks/catechism/.

2) Saint Maria Faustina Kowalska, *Diary: Divine Mercy in My Soul*, 3rd ed. (Stockbridge, MA: Marian Press, 2005).

3) Saint John Paul II, *Theology of the Body* (United States Conference of Catholic Bishops, 1979–84), accessed at https://www.usccb.org/issues-and-action/marriage-and-family/natural-family-planning/catholic-teaching/theology-of-the-body.

4) Anna Amodeo, *No More Holes in My Shoes* (Bloomington, IN: iUniverse, 2012).

5) *Les Misérables*, directed by Tom Hooper, starring Hugh Jackman (Universal City, CA: Universal Pictures, 2012).

6) *The Lion King*, directed by Roger Allers and Rob Minkoff, featuring voice of Matthew Broderick (Burbank, CA: Walt Disney Pictures,1994).

7) Saint Teresa of Avila, *Interior Castle*, trans. E. Alison Peers (New York: Dover, 2008).

8) Ralph A. DiOrio, *Called to Heal: Releasing the Transforming Power of God* (New York: Doubleday, 1982).

9) *The Little Mermaid*, directed by Ron Clements and John Musker, featuring voice of Jodi Benson (Burbank, CA: Walt Disney Pictures, 1989).

10) *Rocky*, directed by John G. Avildsen, starring Sylvester Stallone (Beverly Hills, CA: United Artists, 1976).

ABOUT THE AUTHOR

Joelle Maryn is an award-winning actress, international speaker, and TV host. In her past, she modeled for many national brands, was on a billboard in Times Square, and graced the covers of numerous books and publications.

Several years ago, Joelle had a miraculous conversion experience and now shares her message of God's healing love around the world. She also engages in faith-based, inspirational, and family-friendly films and TV shows to help lead others closer to Christ.

Joelle recently produced, co-wrote, and starred in the award-winning film *Fully Known*. And as host of Shalom World TV's *Beyond the Vision*, she has been blessed to interview many celebrities and public figures. In addition, Joelle has appeared on several international podcasts, radio, and TV shows, including *The Journey Home* on EWTN.

When she's not on camera or at speaking engagements, Joelle's favorite things are walking on the beach, watching sunrises and sunsets, singing, dancing like no one is watching, and spending time with family, especially her beloved children.

www.ingramcontent.com/pod-product-compliance
Lightning Source LLC
Chambersburg PA
CBHW051510150726
47997CB00001B/188